East End Photos

Through Mayar's Eyes

Photo Album: Bancroft BBQ 31.8.2007

MAYAR AKASH

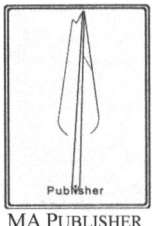

Publisher

MA PUBLISHER

The right of Mayar Akash to be identified as the author of this work has been asserted in accordance with sections 77 and 78 of the Copyright Design and Patent Act 1988.

Published by MA Publishing (Penzance) 2020
Published December 2020
ISBN-13: 978-1-910499-64-1

Cover designed by Mayar Akash
Typeset in Times New Roman
All photos belong to Mayar Akash

 Paper printed on is FSC Certified, lead free, acid free, buffered paper made from wood-based pulp. Our paper meets the ISO 9706 standard for permanent paper. As such, paper will last several hundred years when stored.

Introduction

This is 6th photo books of the series featuring photos from Tower Hamlets which, I've taken over the years growing up in the East End of London. When I first got my first camera in the late 80's, as I grew and my curiosity my ideas changed and formed; and I started snapping away where my tenacity drew me. Today I present those photos captured through "My Eyes," the environment had changed along with the people and social issues, they all had a bearing on my world.

For many years I didn't know what to do with them but now it seems fit to organise them like an albums and publish them, give access to the world, to see the East End through a Bangladeshi, Sylheti living in Tower Hamlets, with the urban factor; no hold bars assimilation into the Cockney East End, perspective.

These photos are not in any particular order, I want to give people a taster of random things that I have encounter in my life journey.

This collection is of an event taken place in 31st of August 2007, at Bancroft estate that I was living at the time. The "Tenants Management Organisation" and the residents put on a "fun day," for the estate residents. These photos are from a resident's perspective taken from home, where I had a good vantage point.

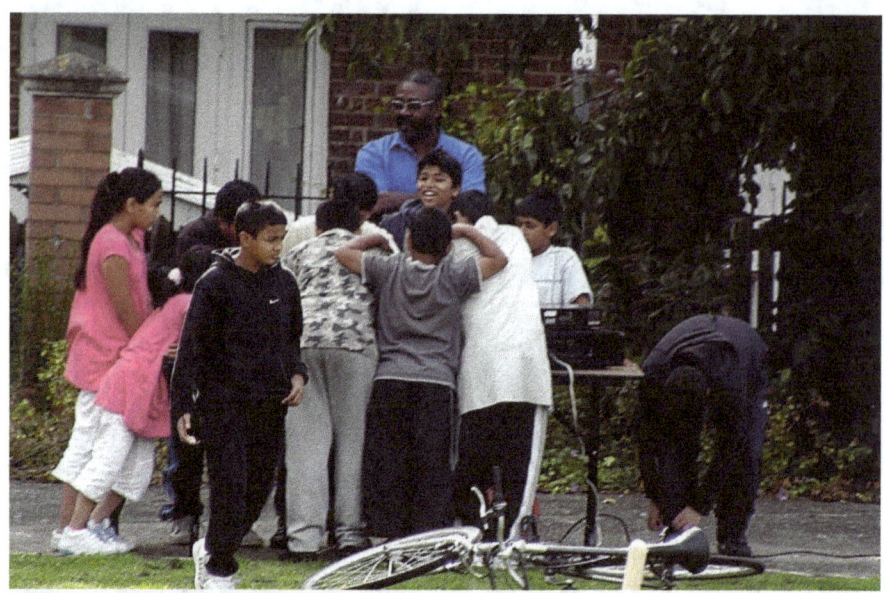

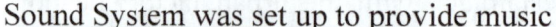
Sound System was set up to provide music

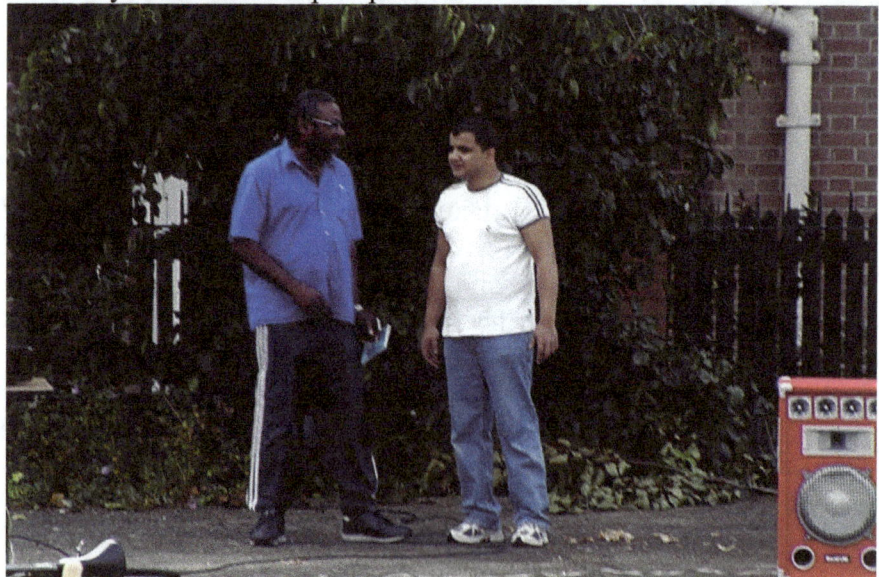

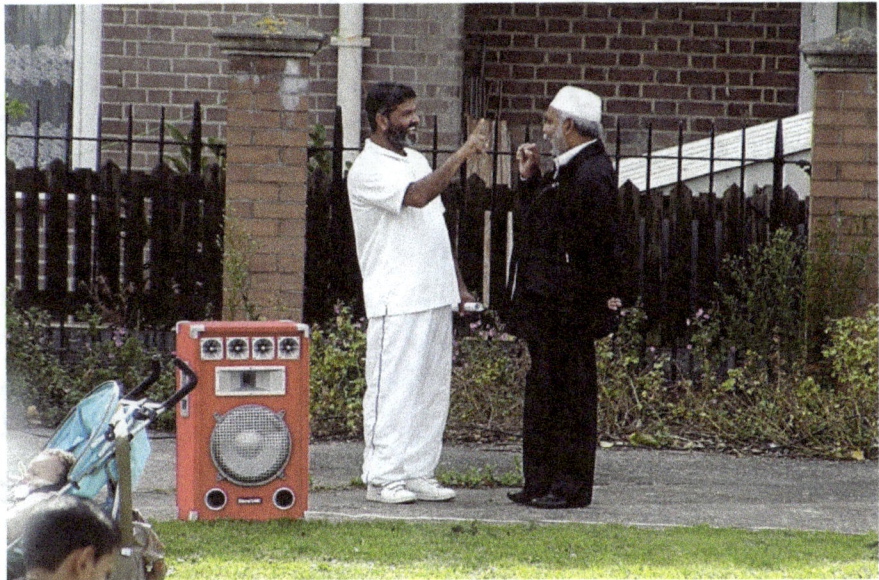

Residents out

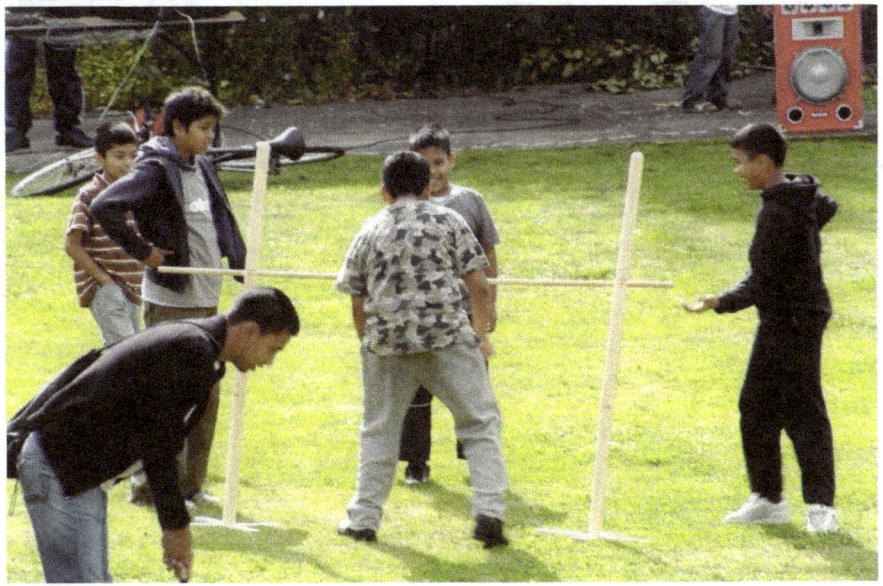

Various games for the young people.

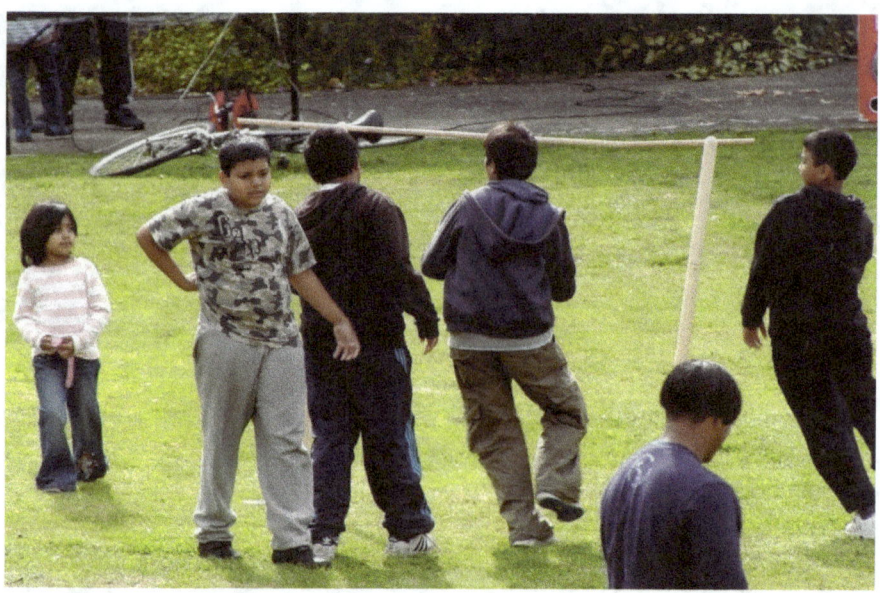

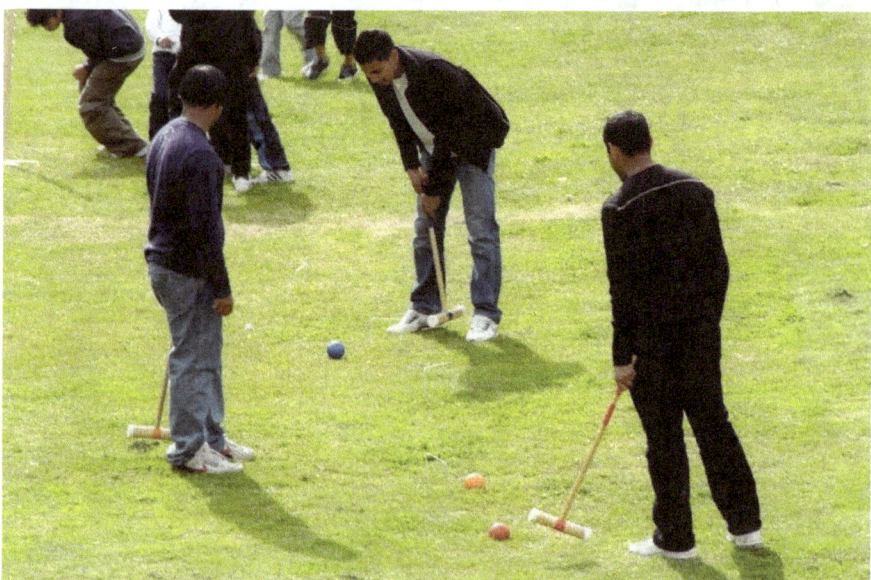

Some British games

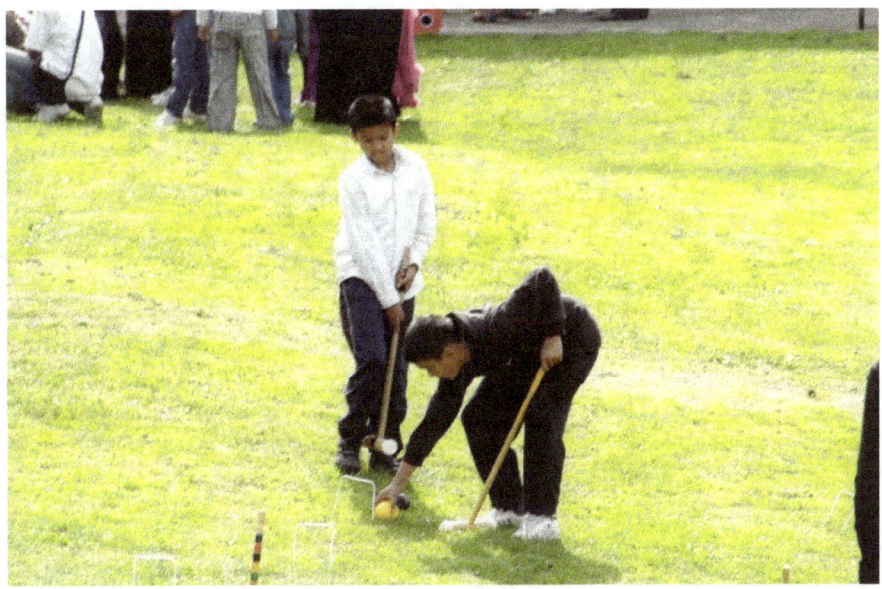

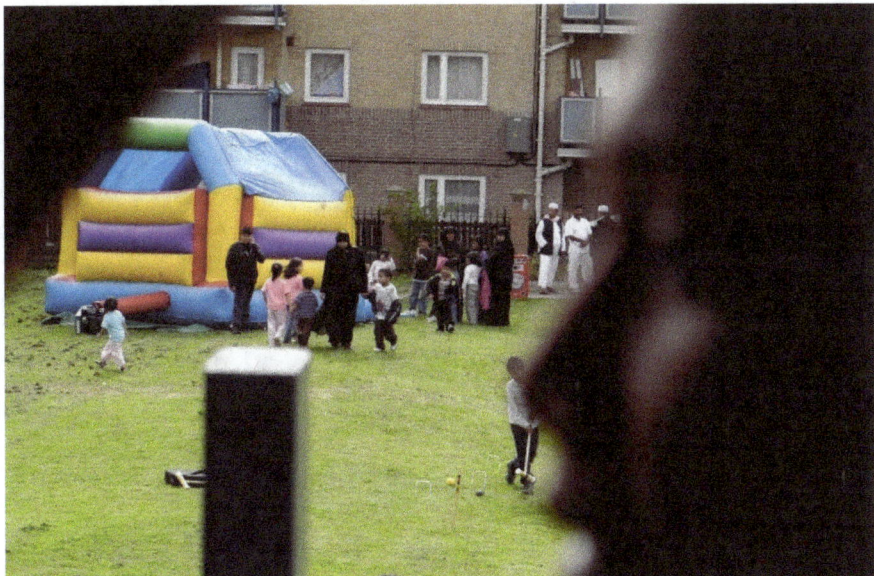

Bouncy Castle for the children.

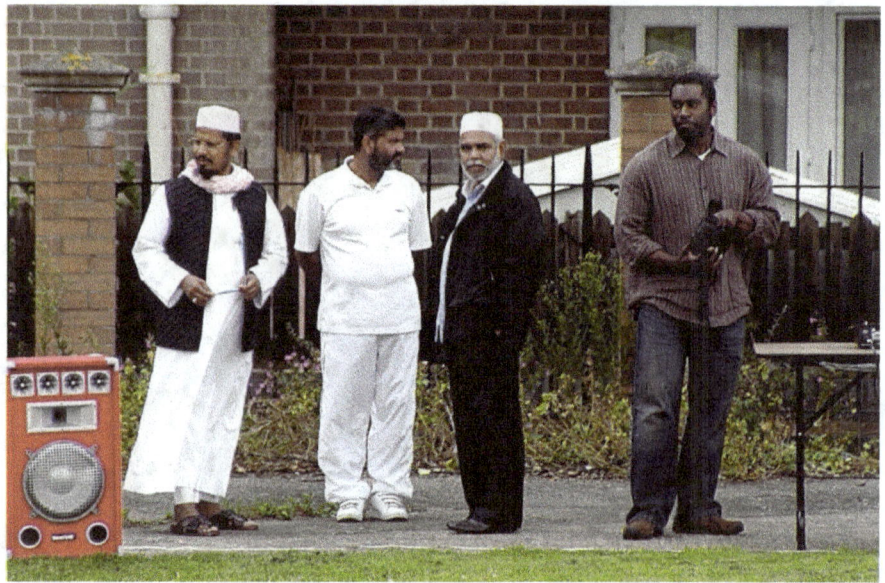

Management members

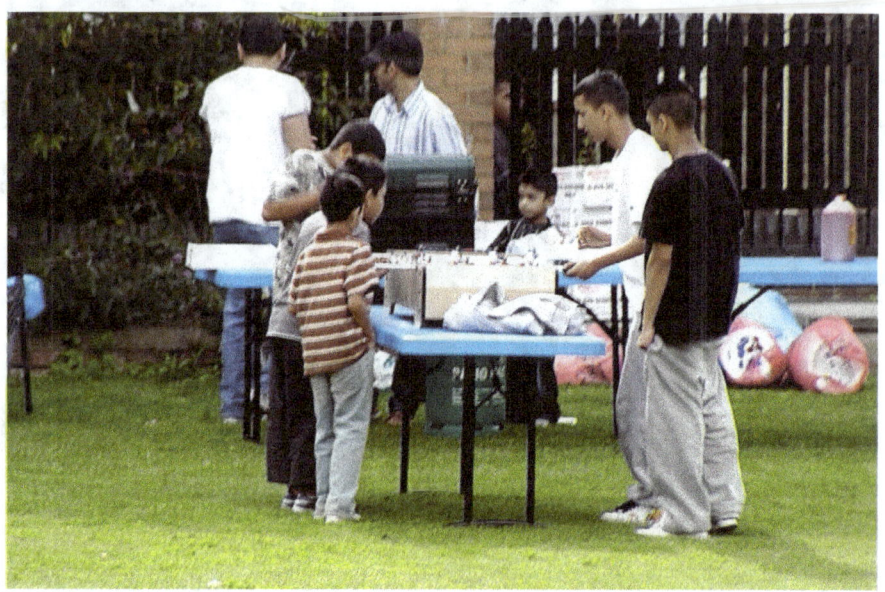

Table top football

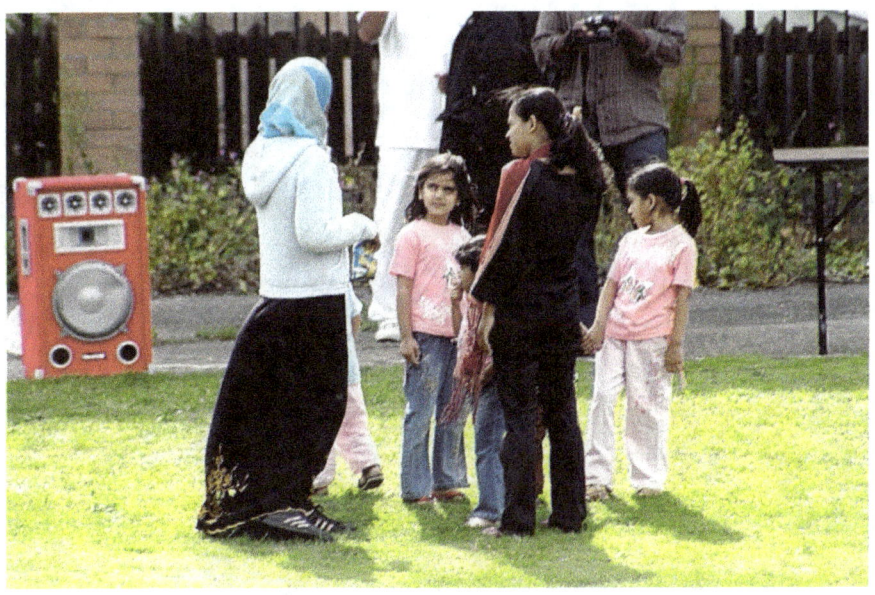

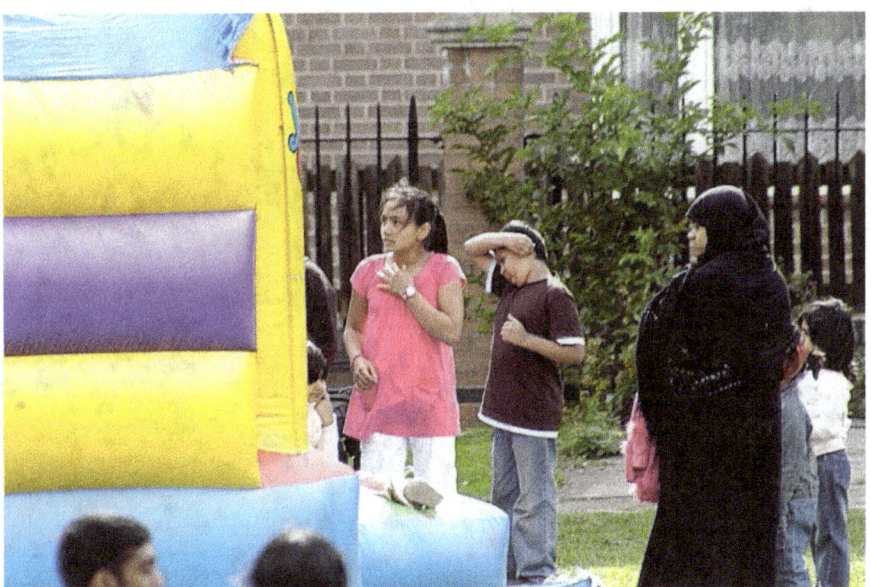

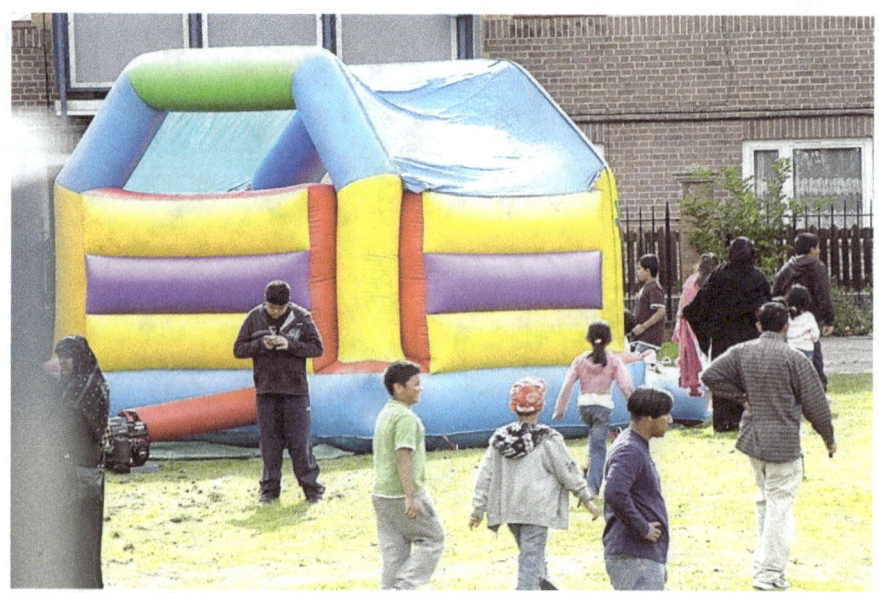

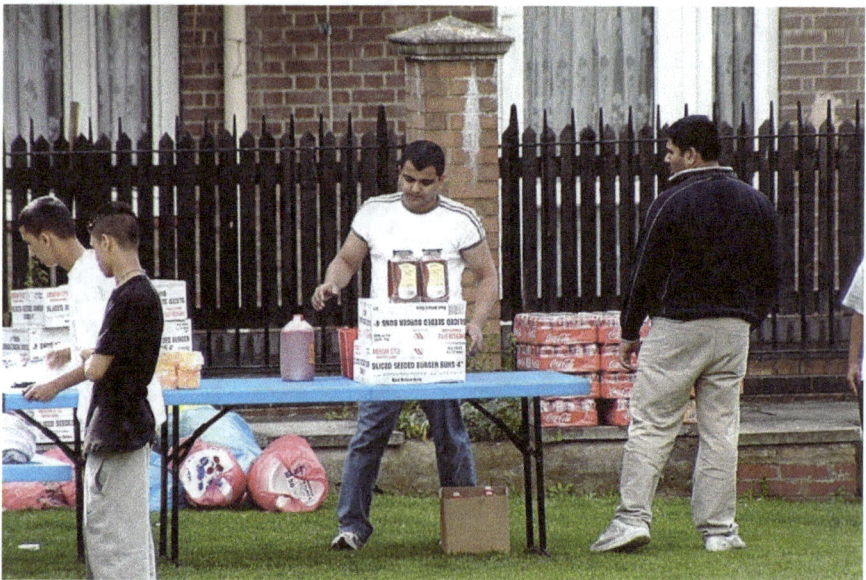

Setting up the BBQ for lunch, Afzal on the ball, getting the food sorted.

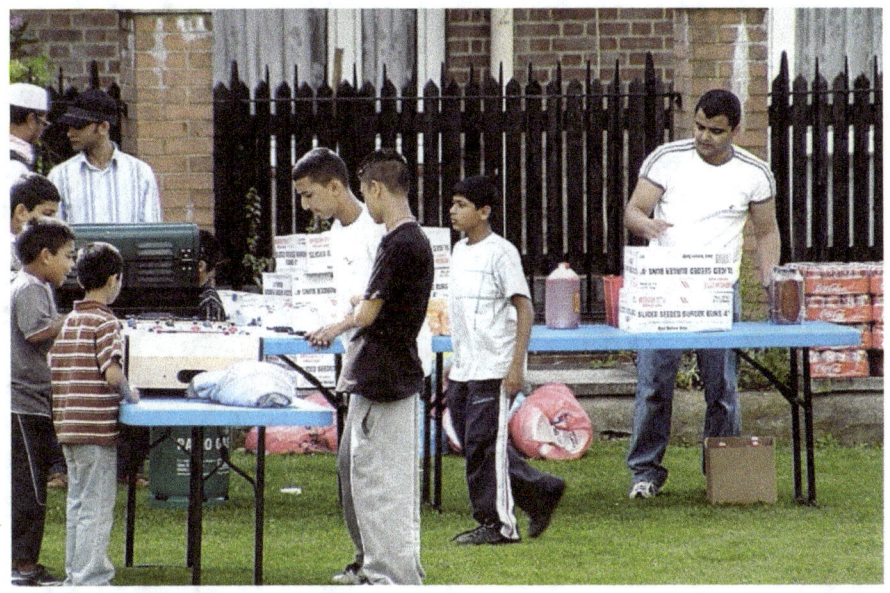

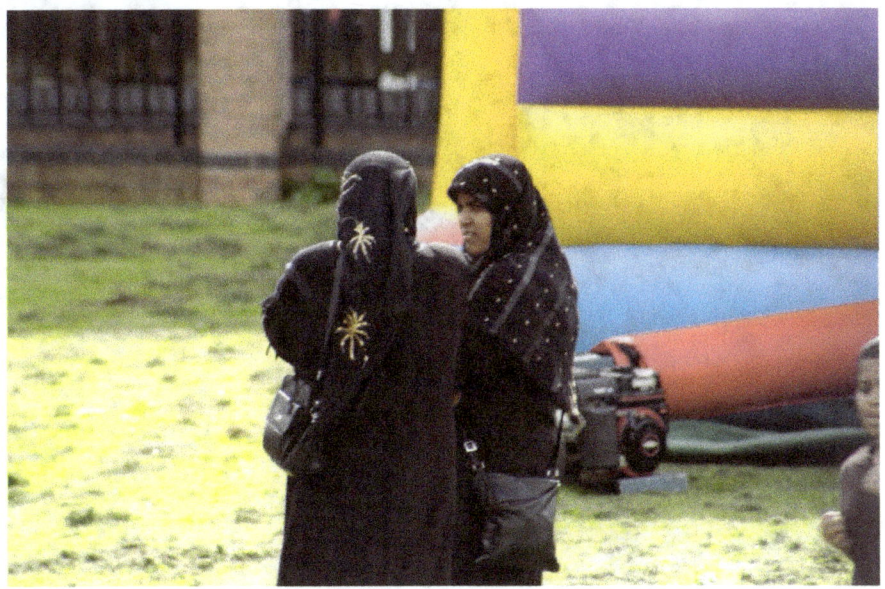

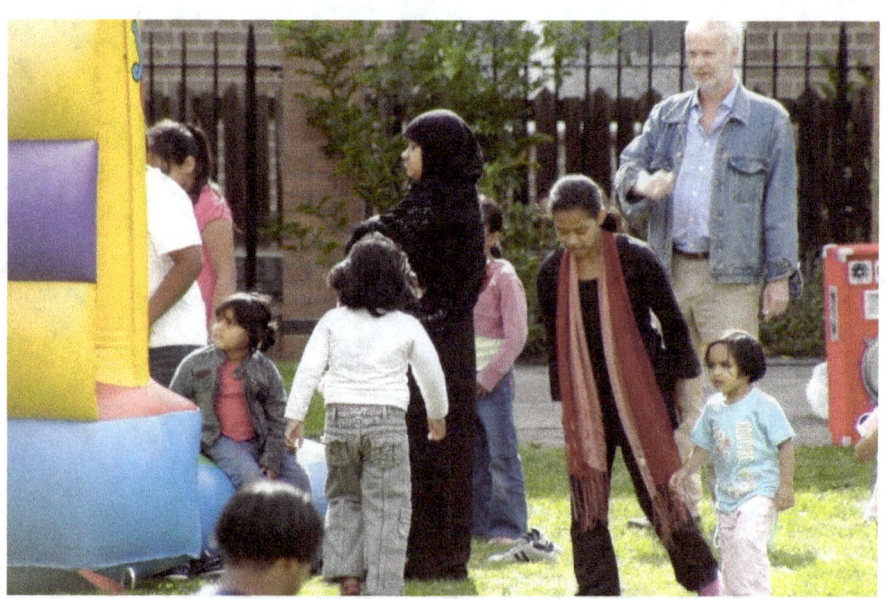

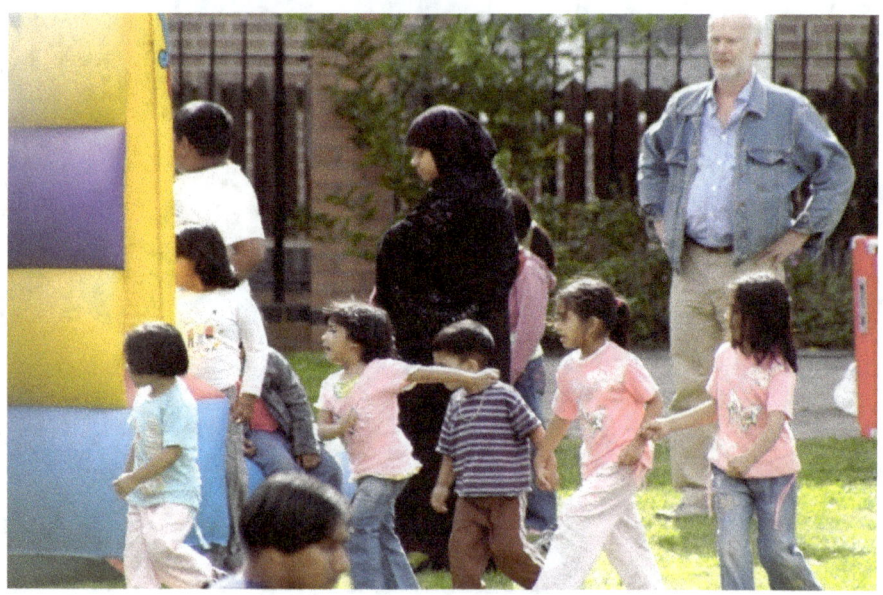

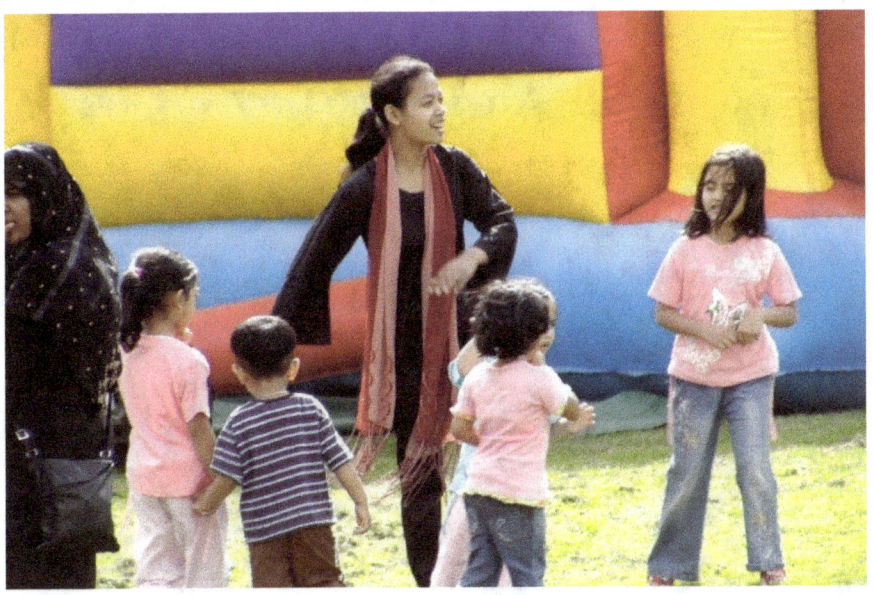

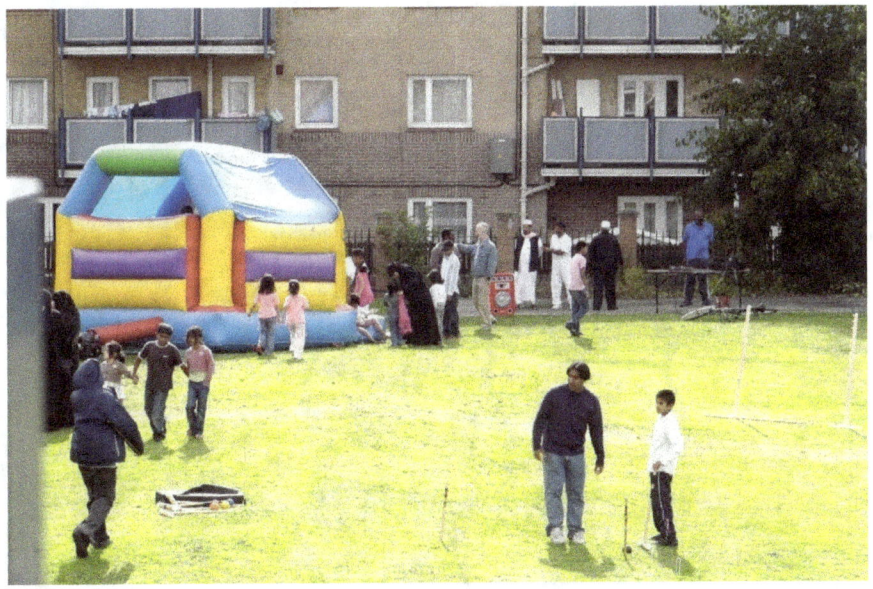

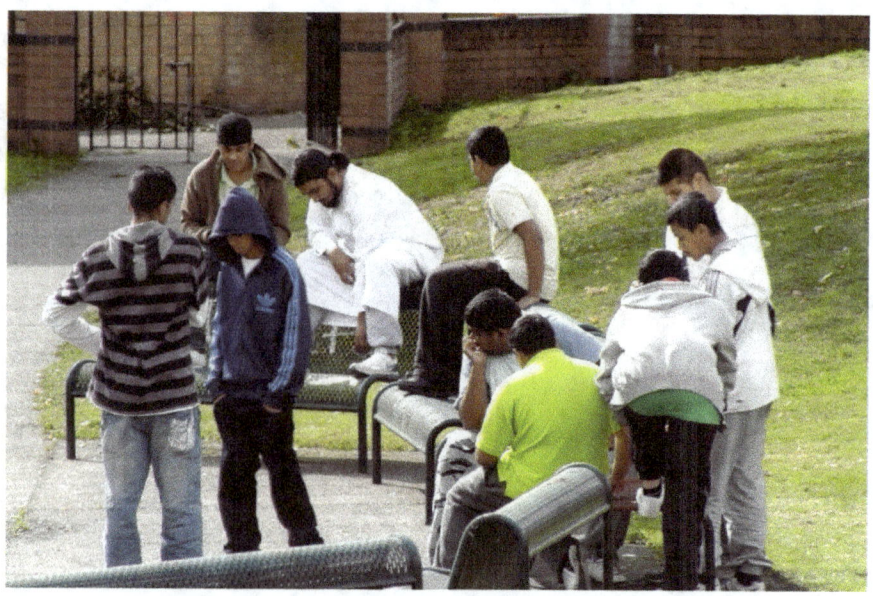

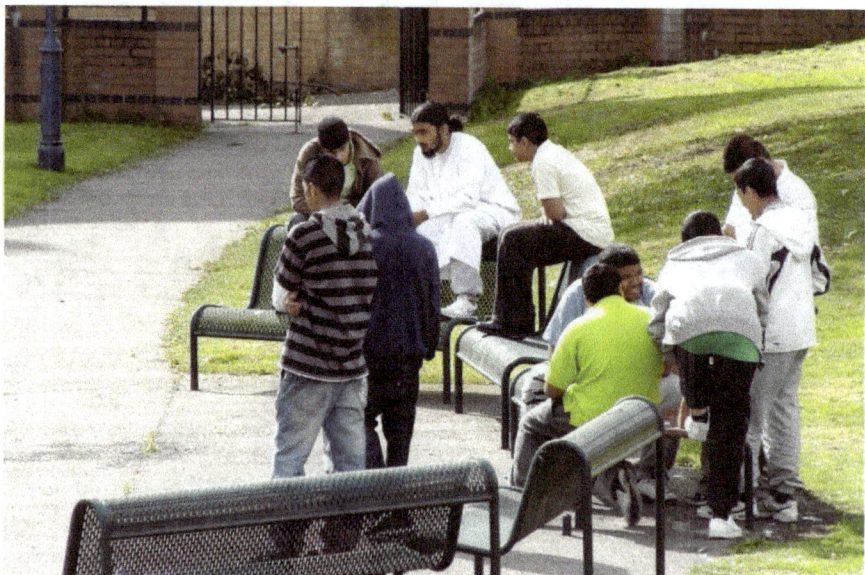

Teenagers gathered to share the experience

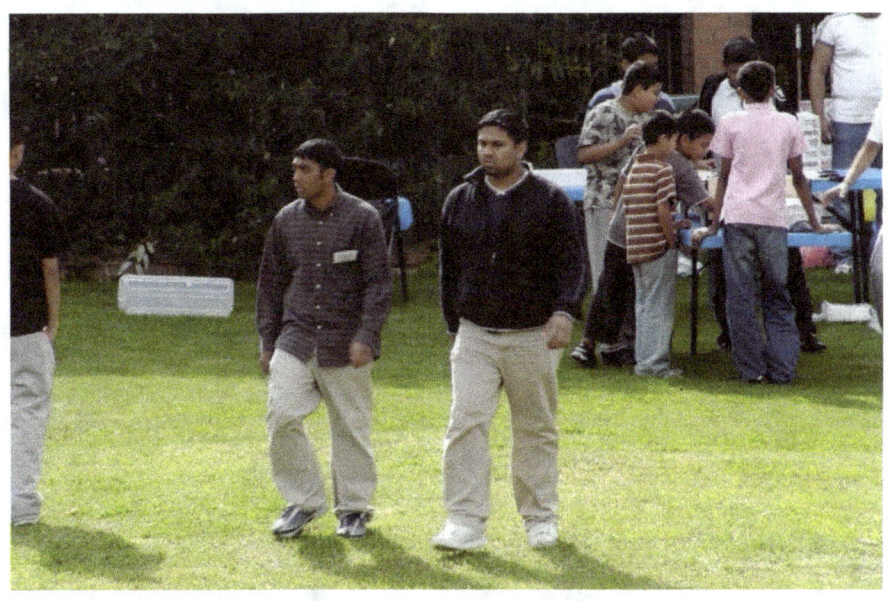

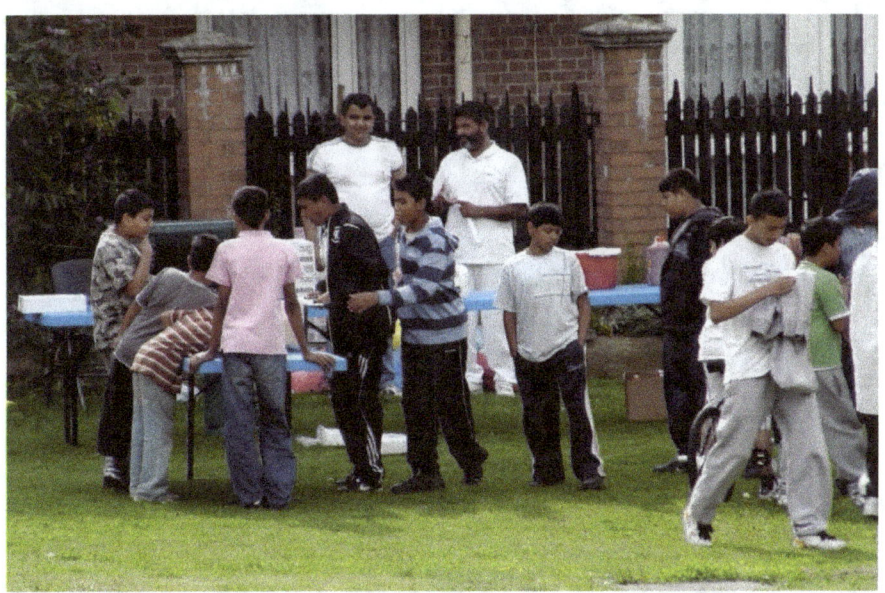

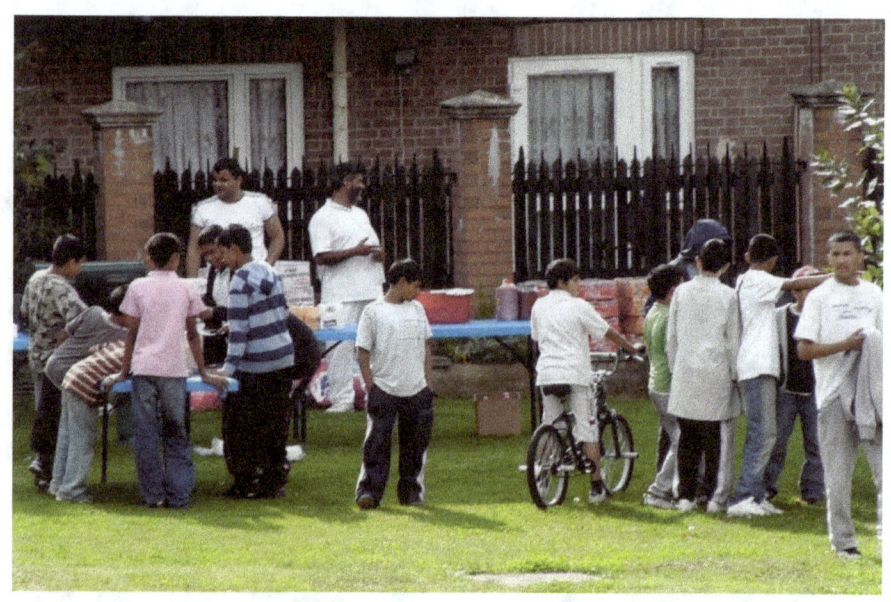

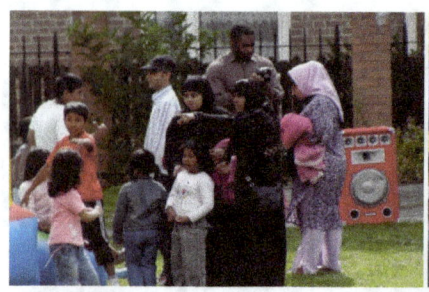
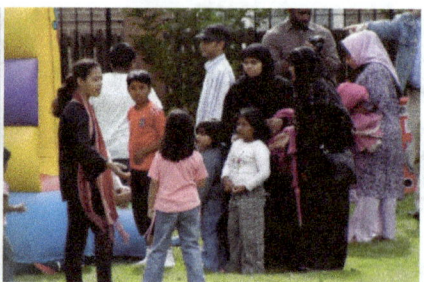

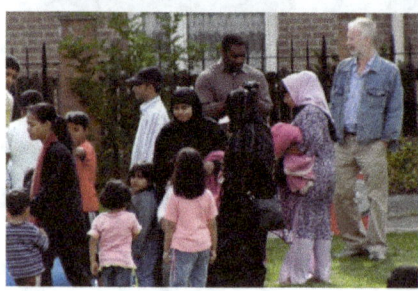
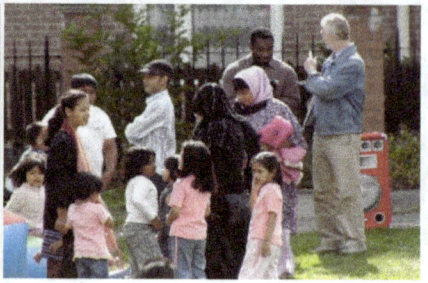

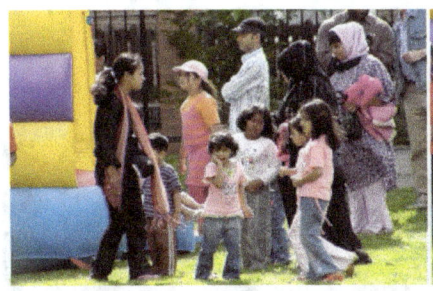
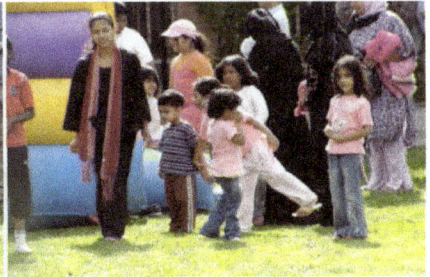
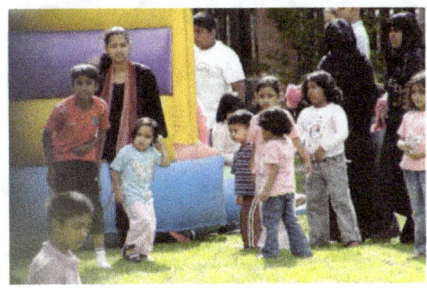
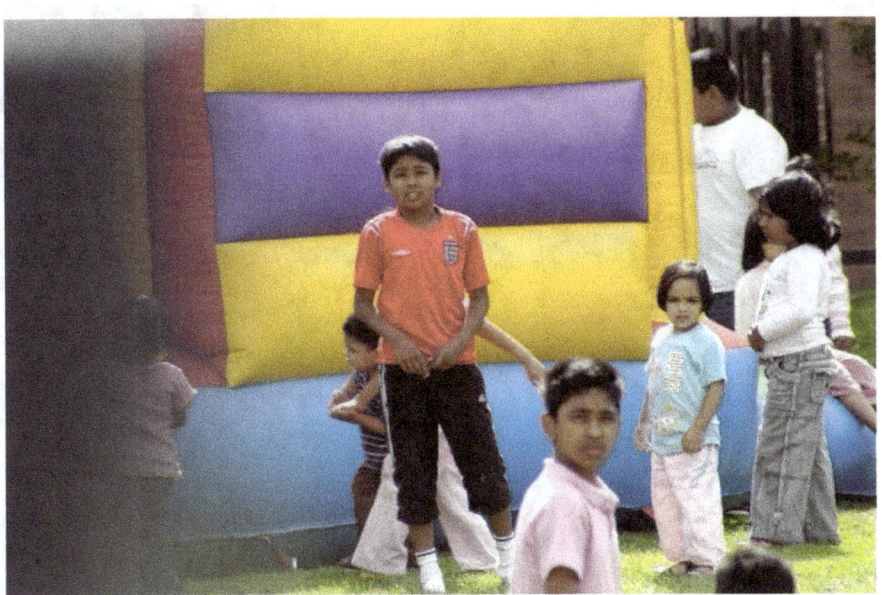

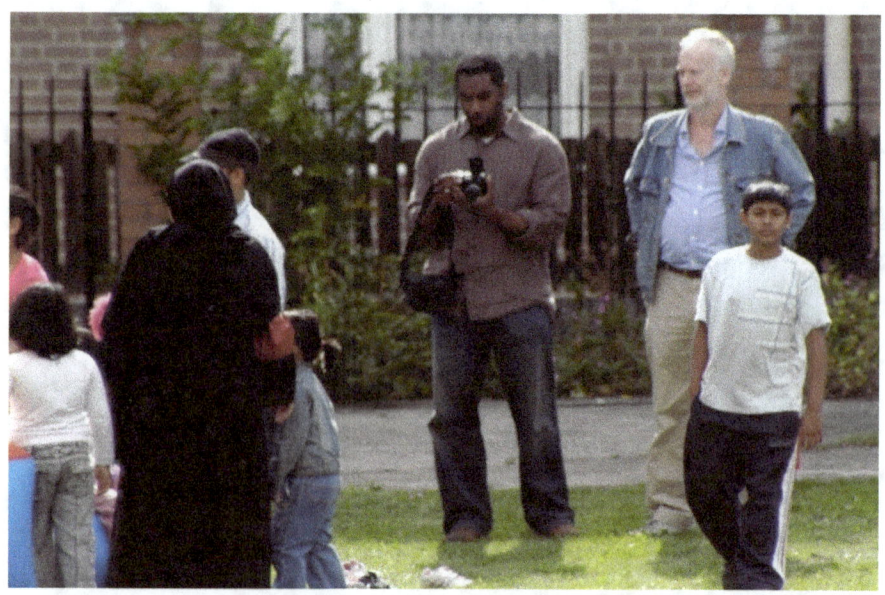

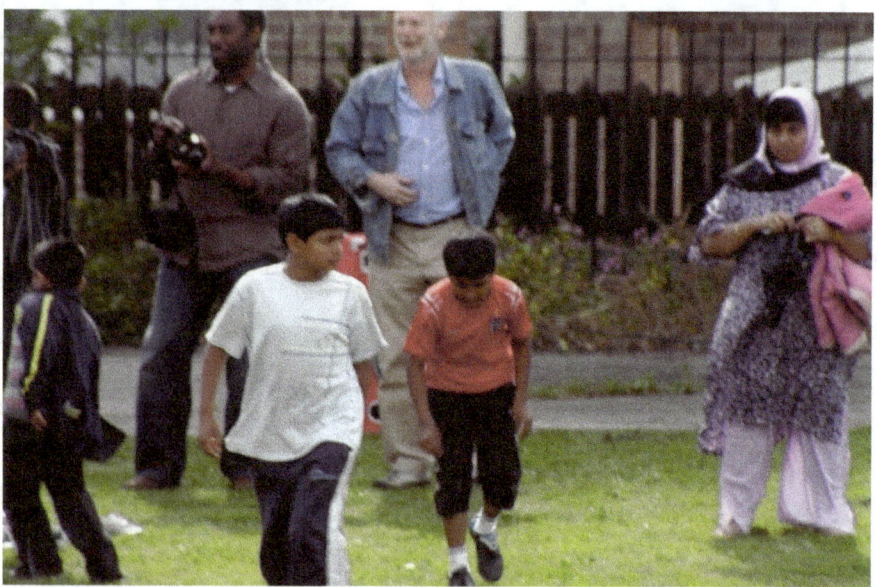

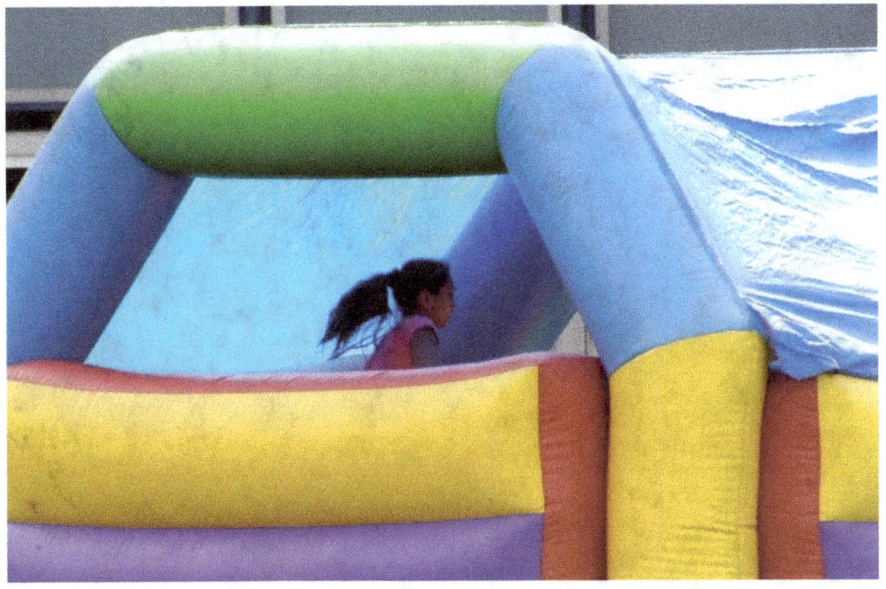

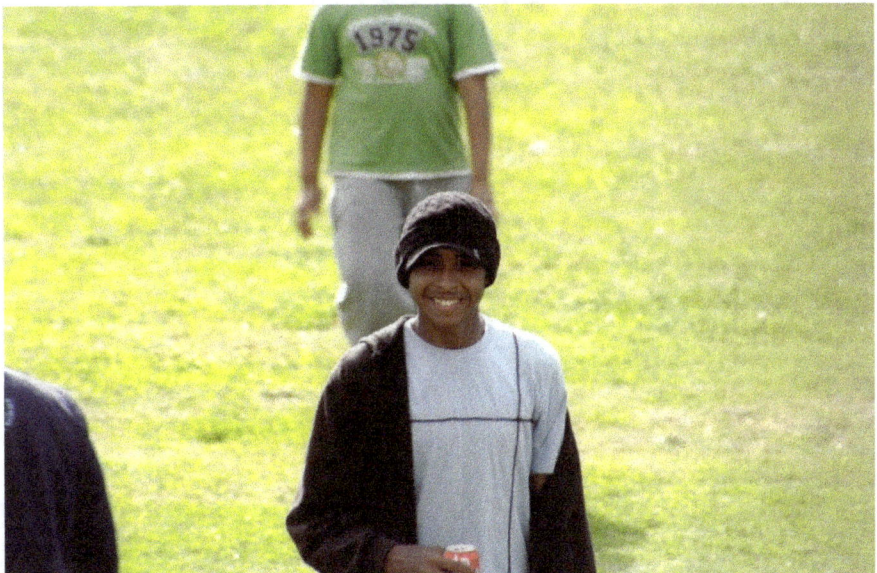

Fun packed and happy experiences

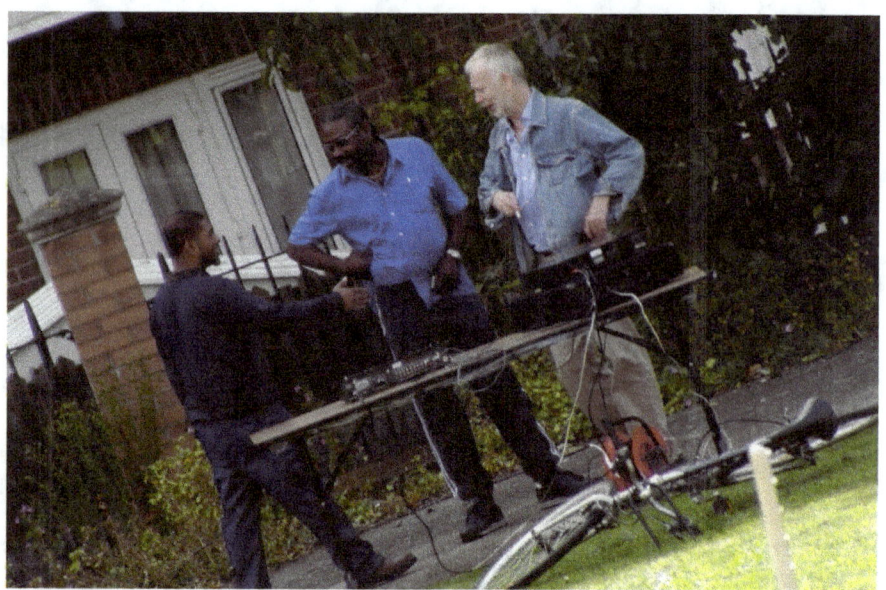

TMO people

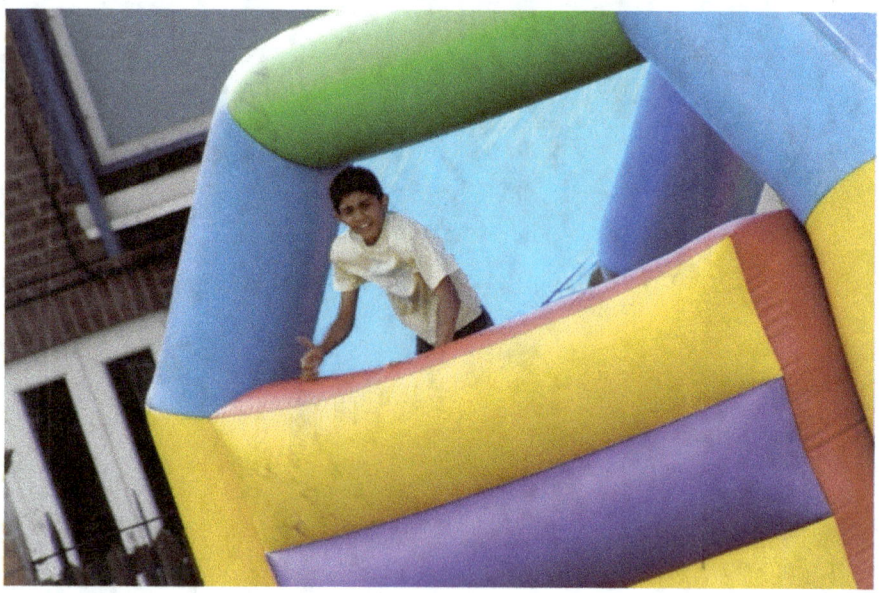

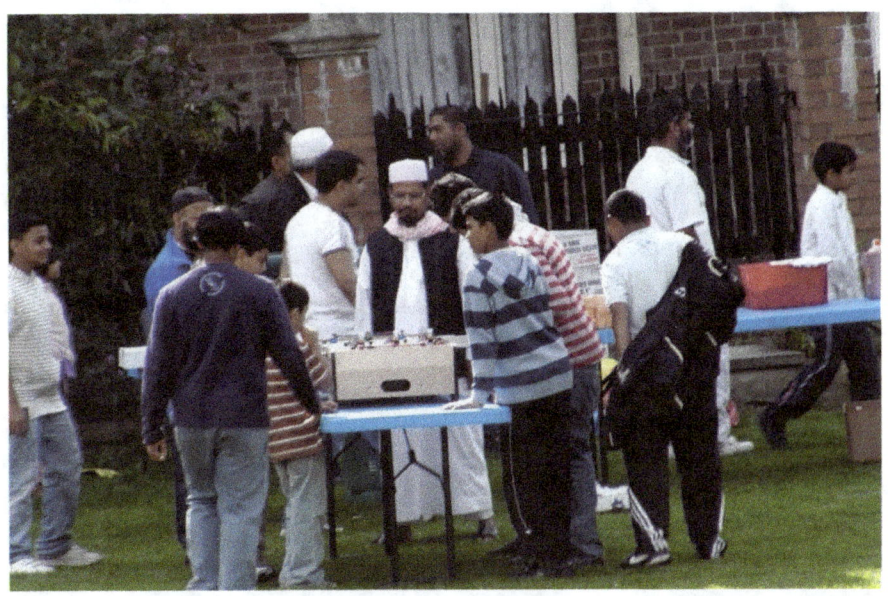

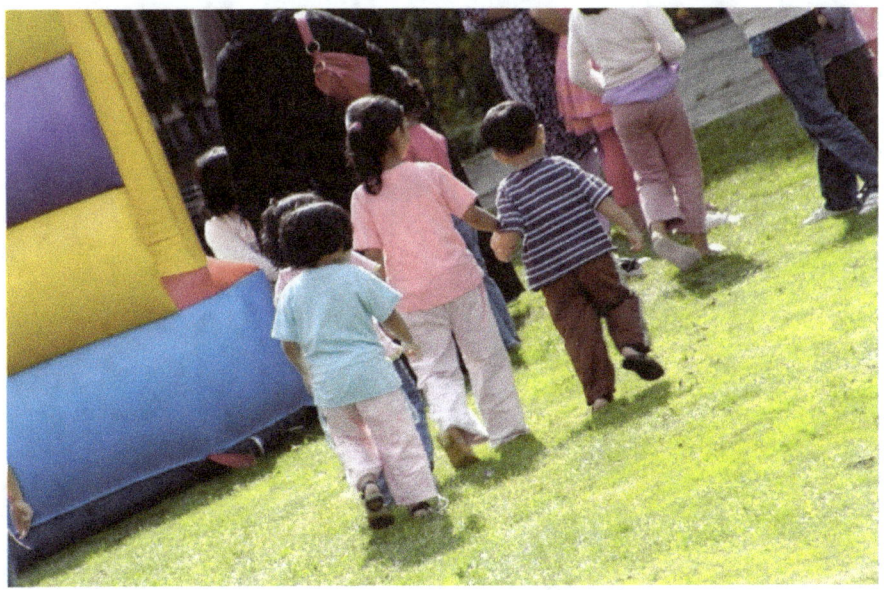

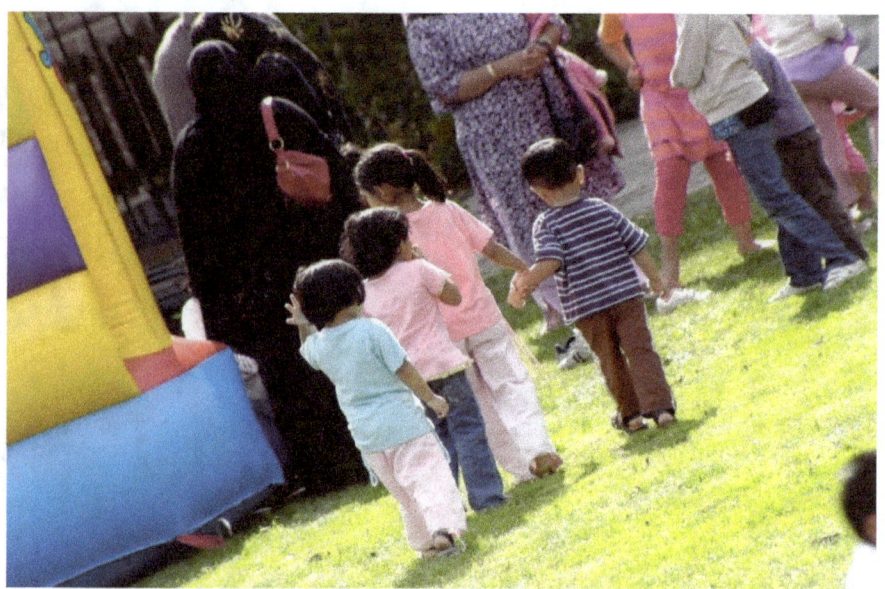

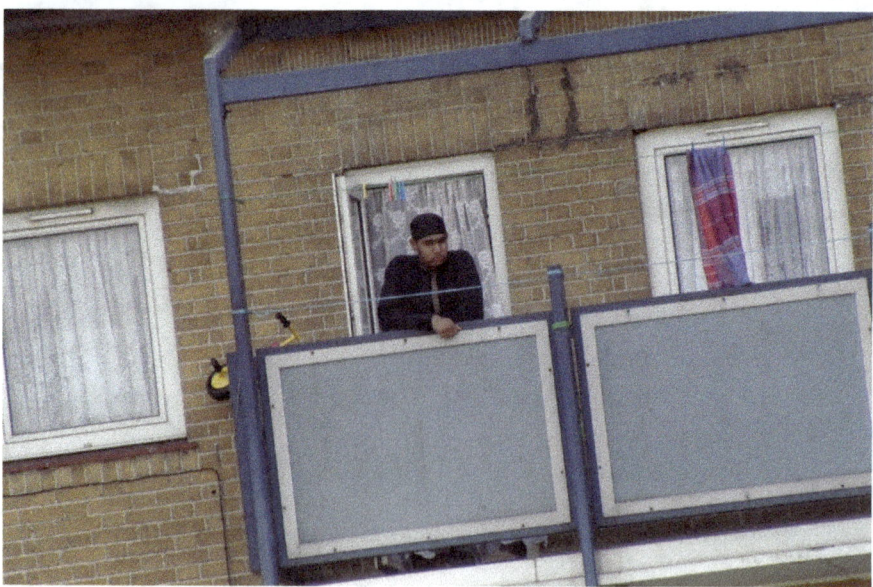

Observing from home

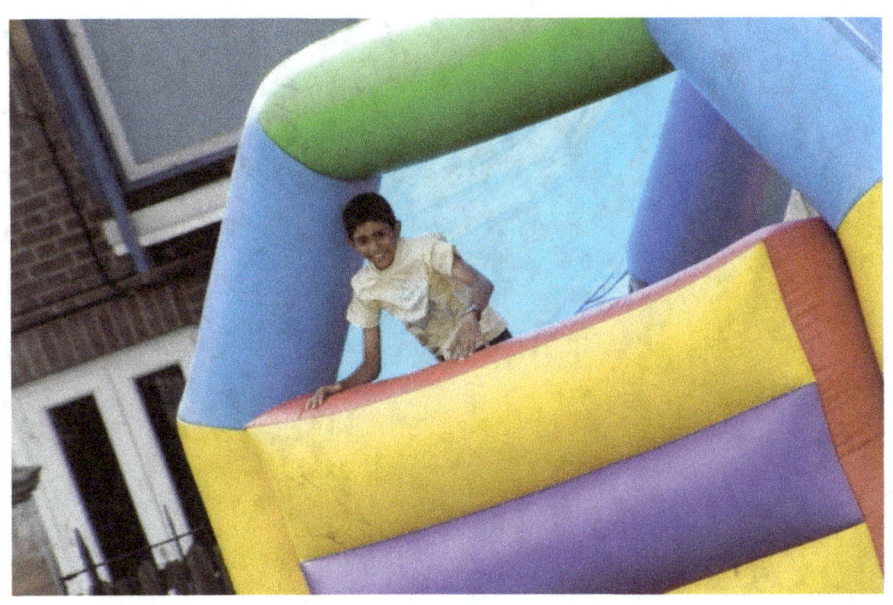

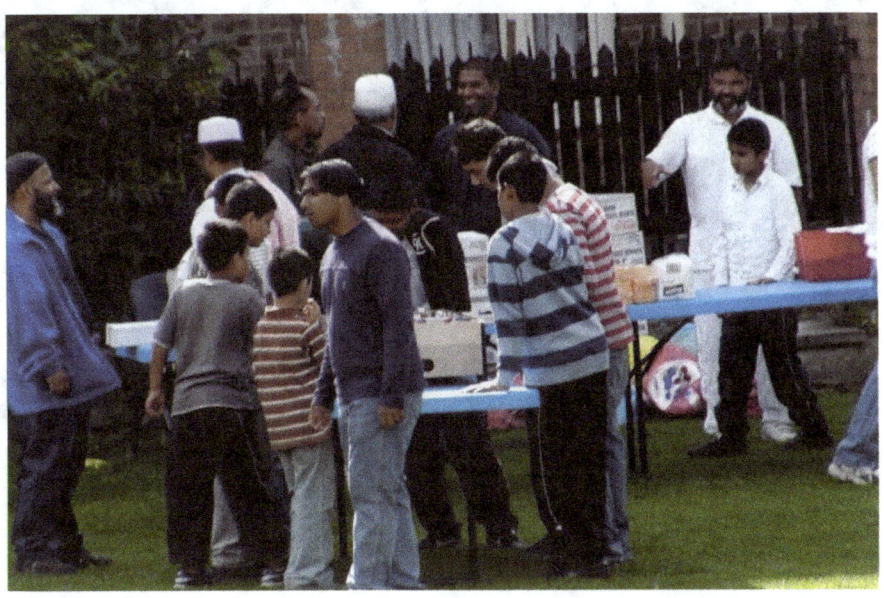

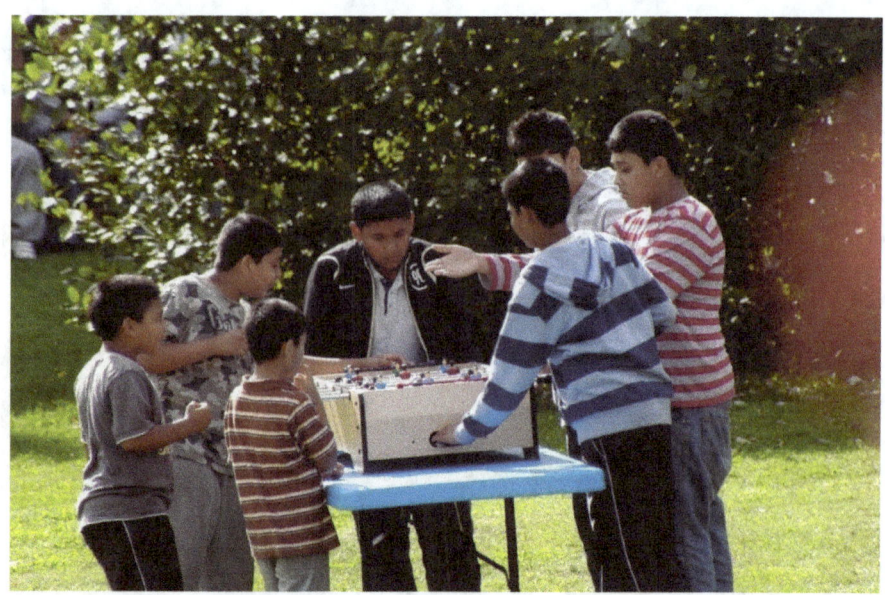

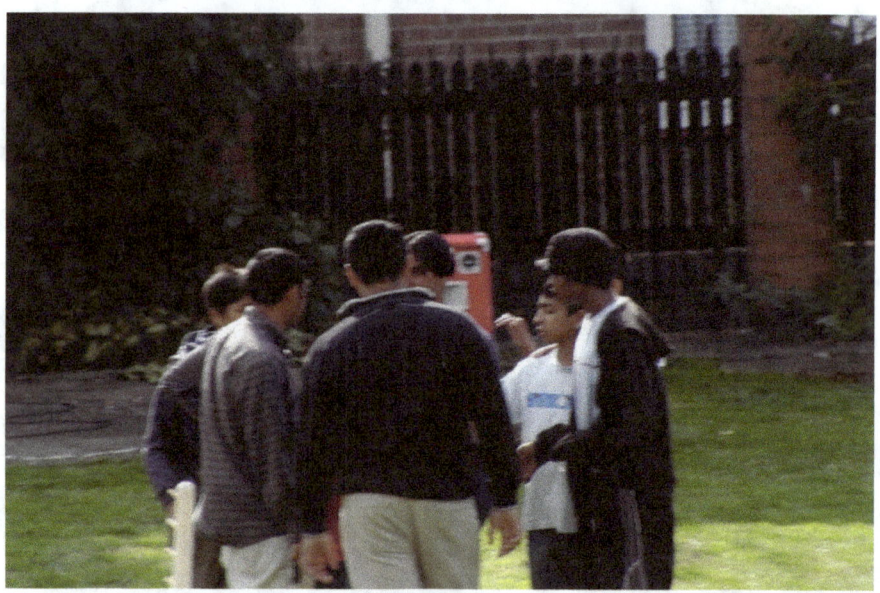

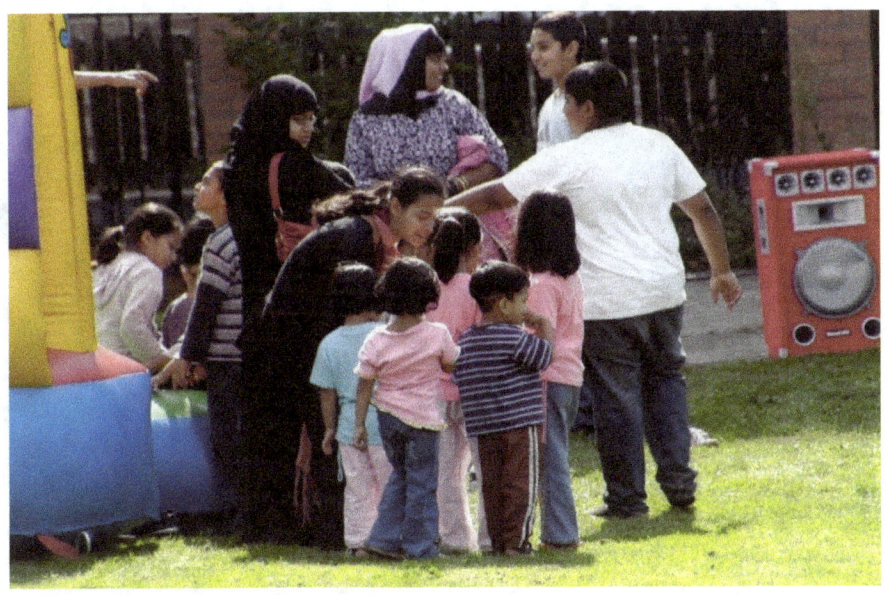

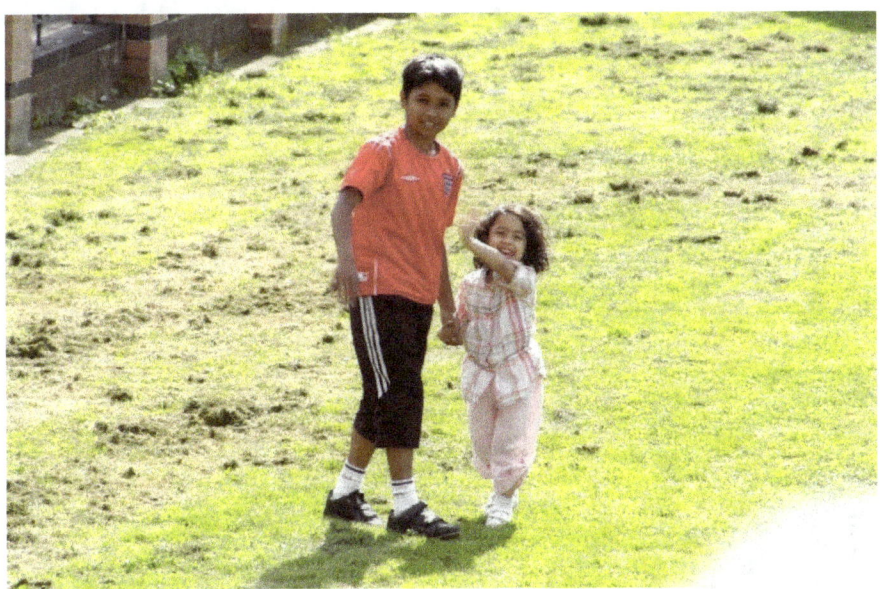

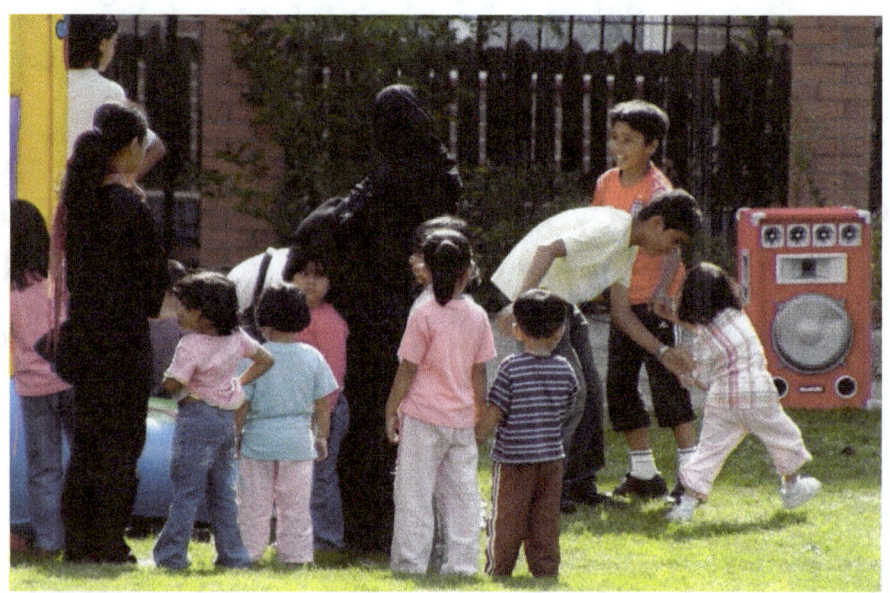

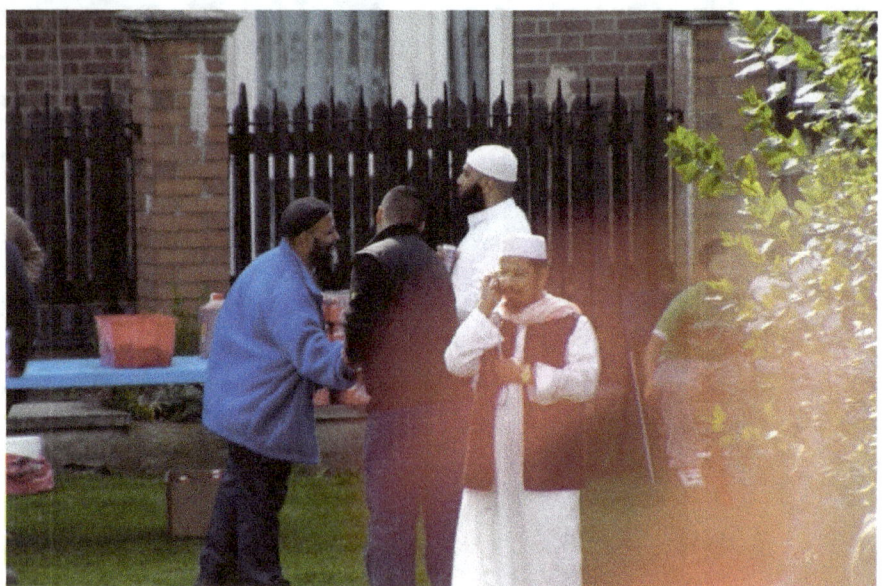

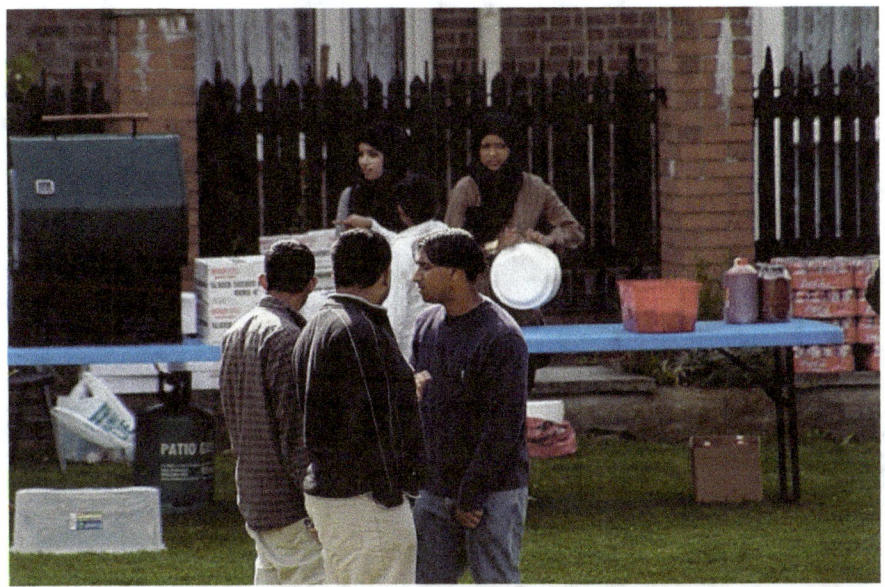

Female team members setting up the BBQ

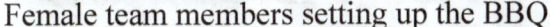

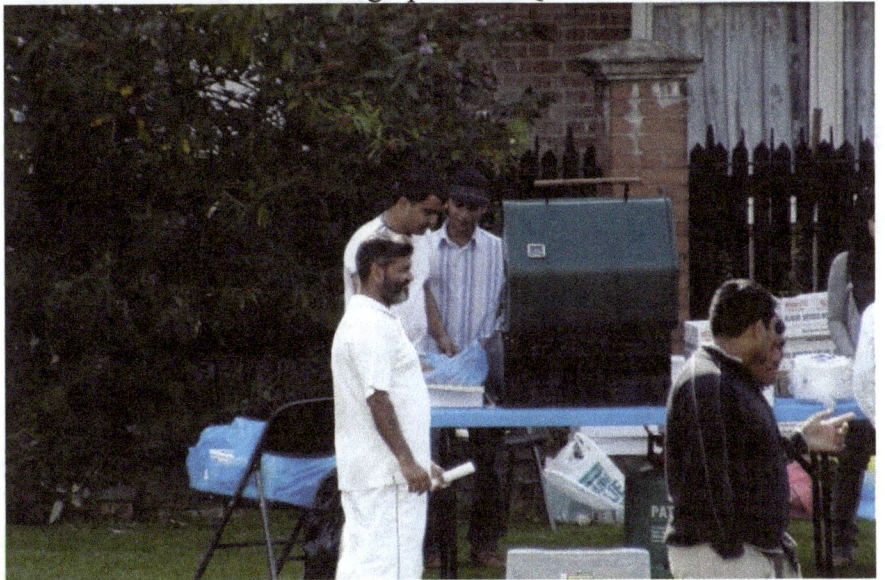

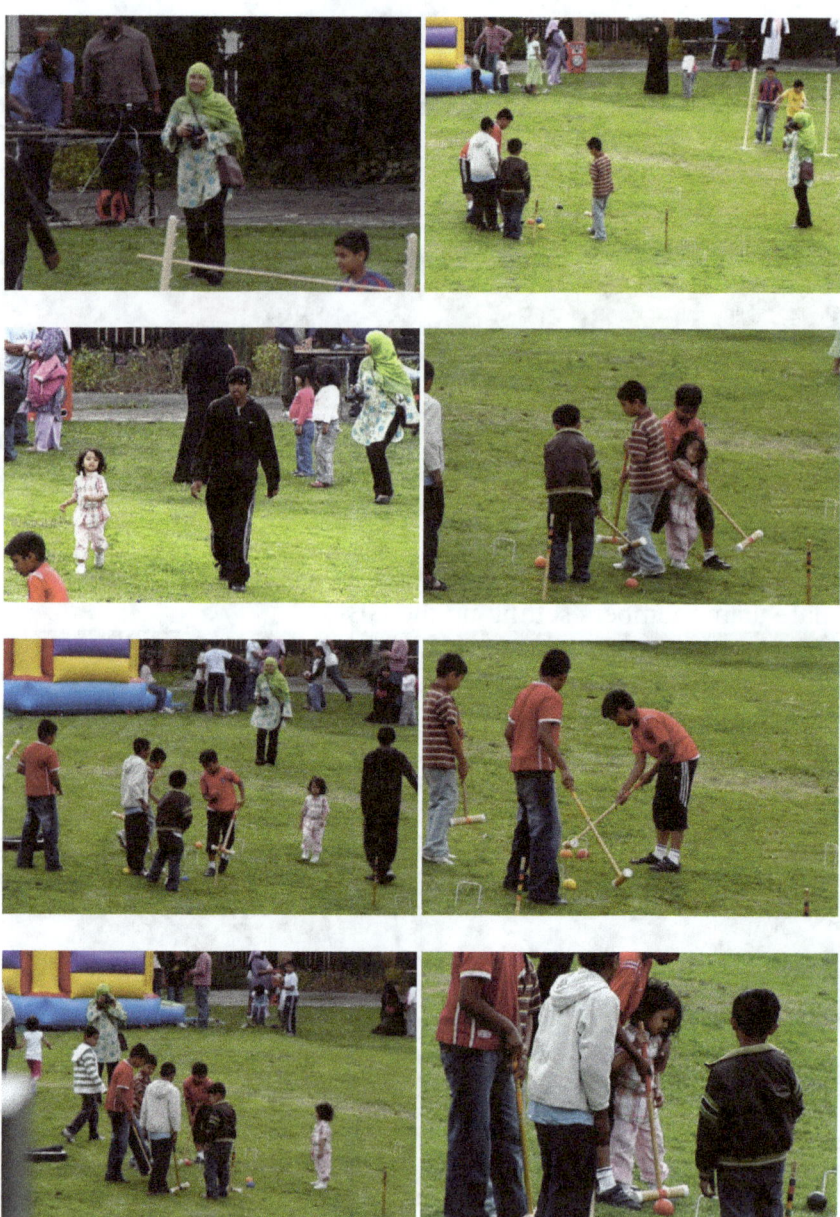

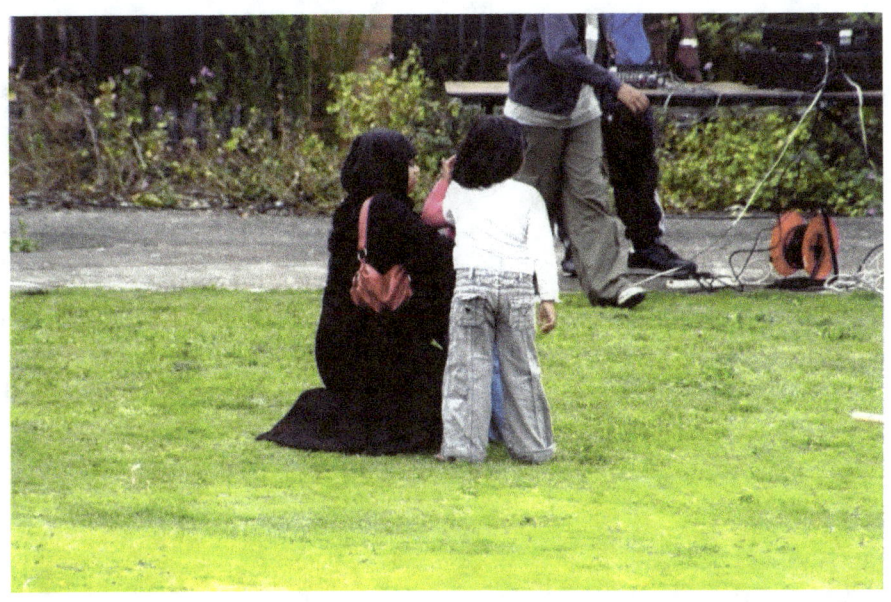

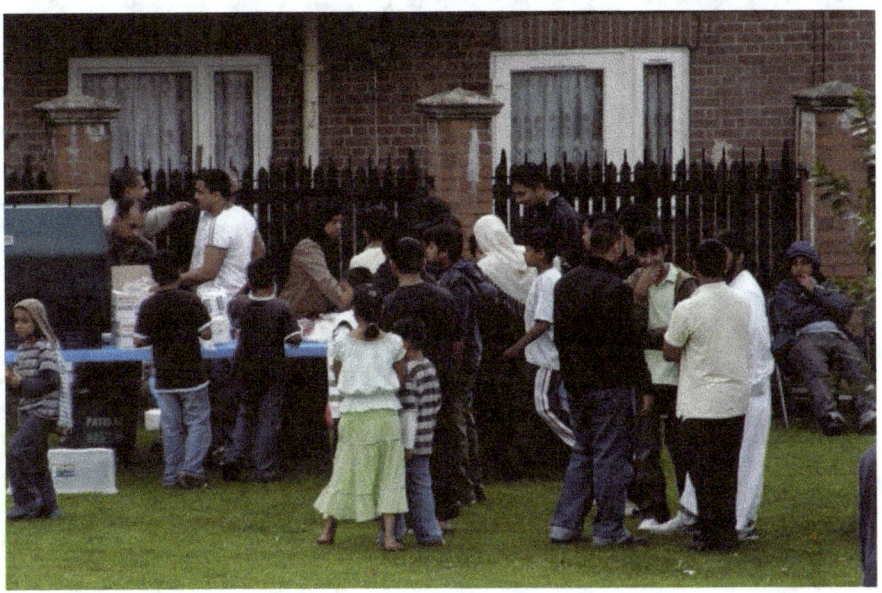

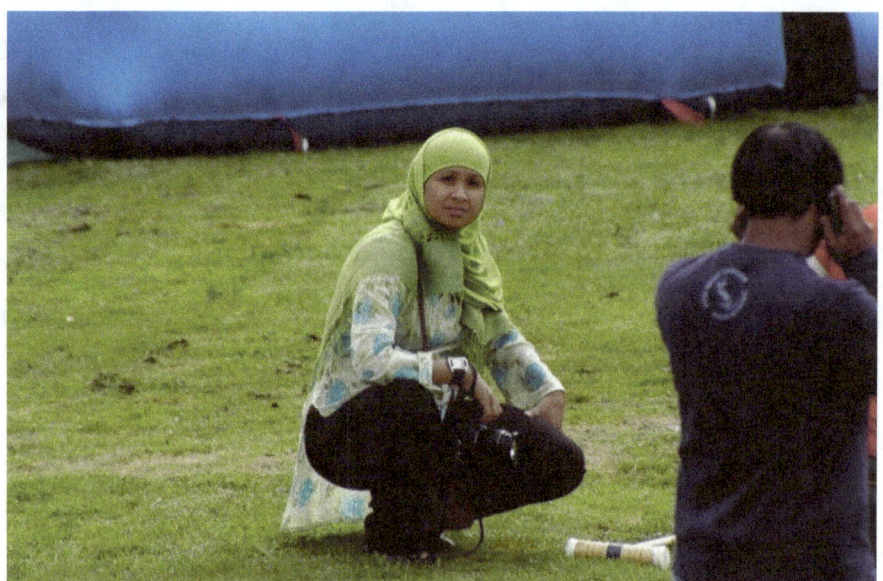

Another photographer capturing the mood of the event

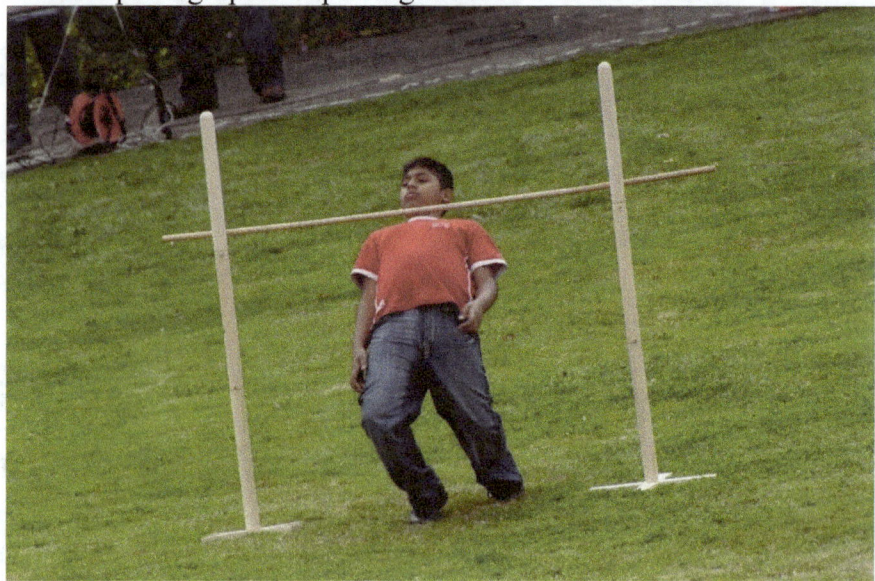

Another game to try

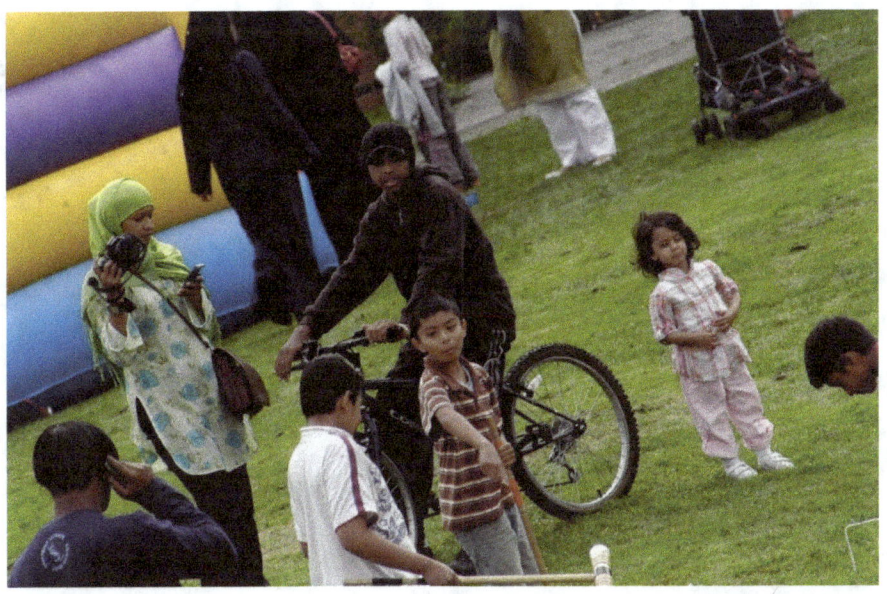

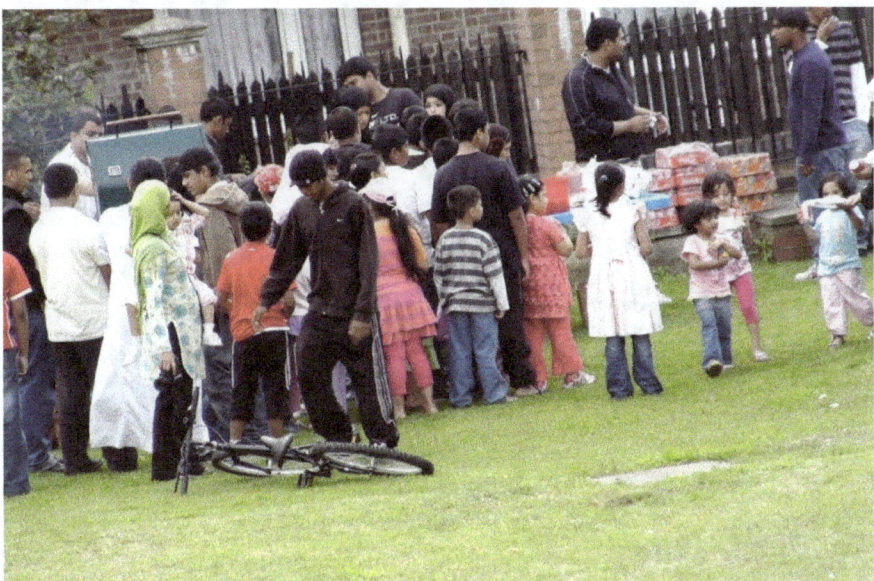

A long wait for at the BBQ stand

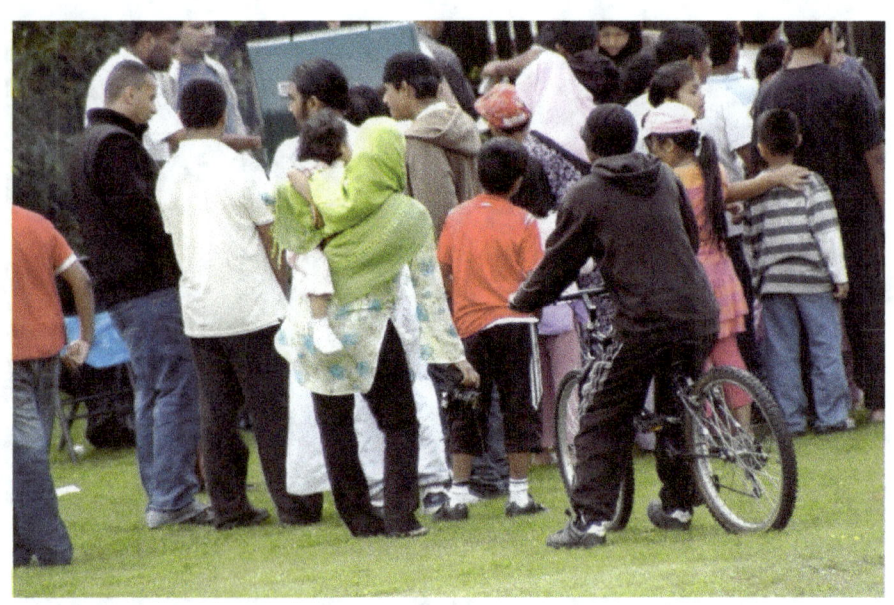

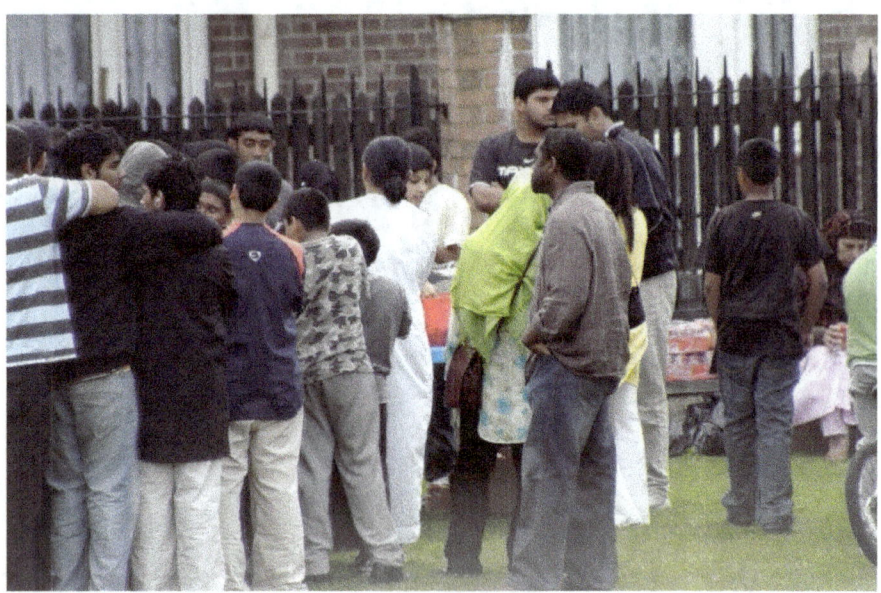

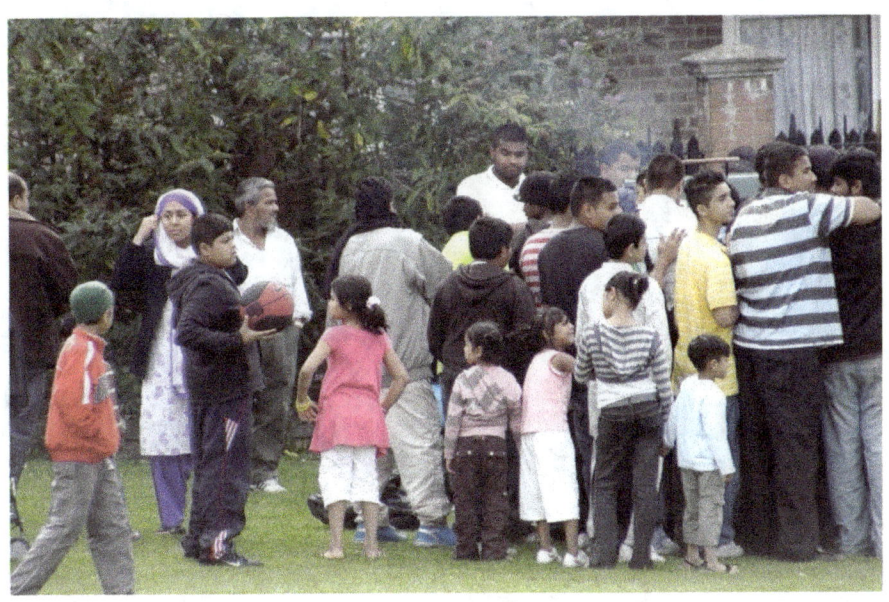

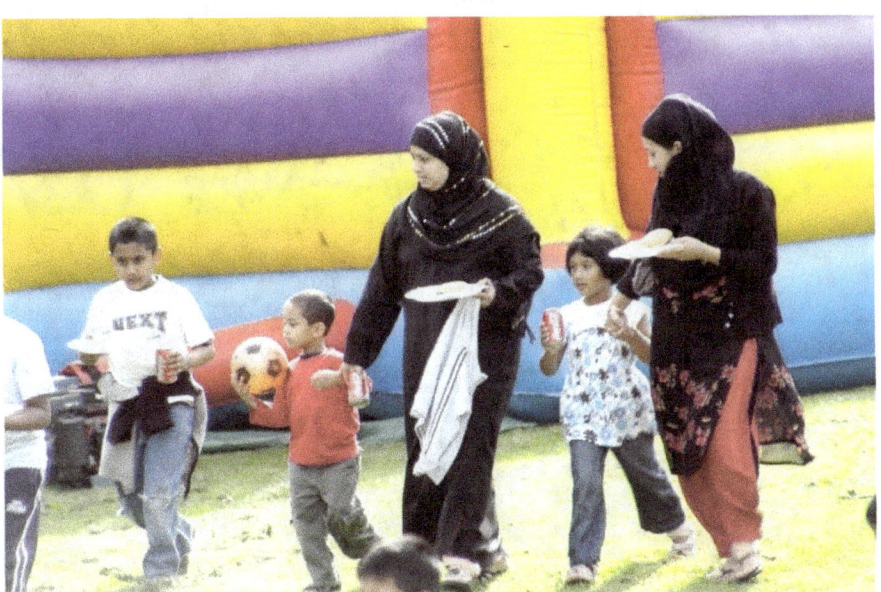

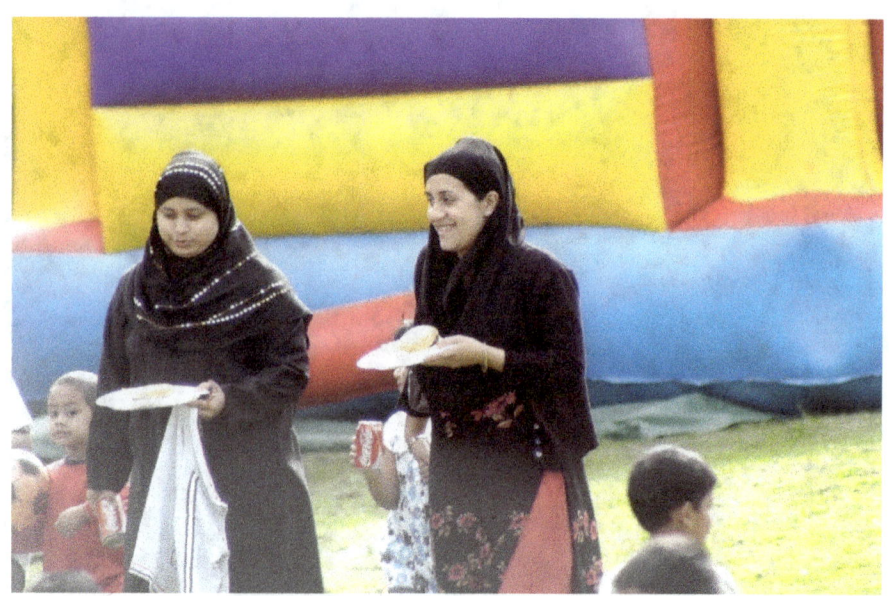

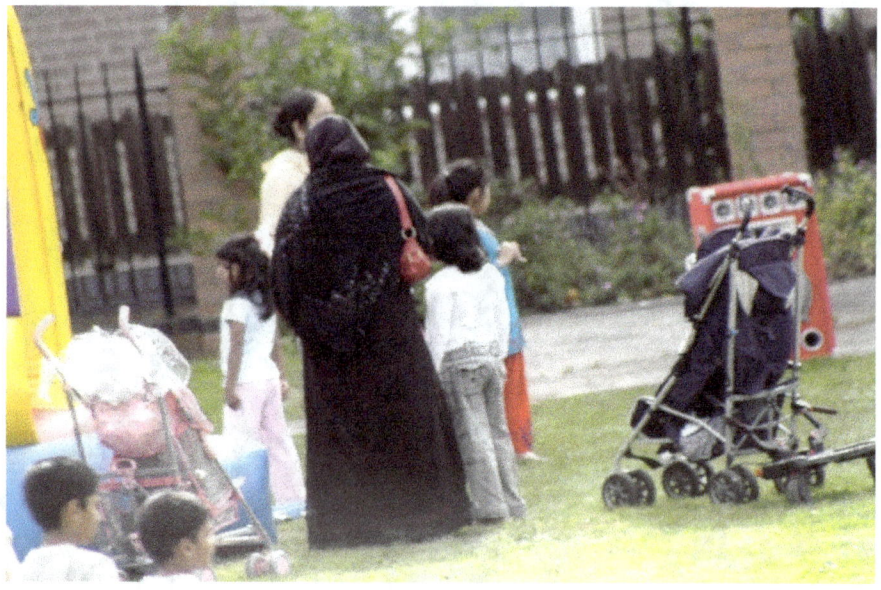

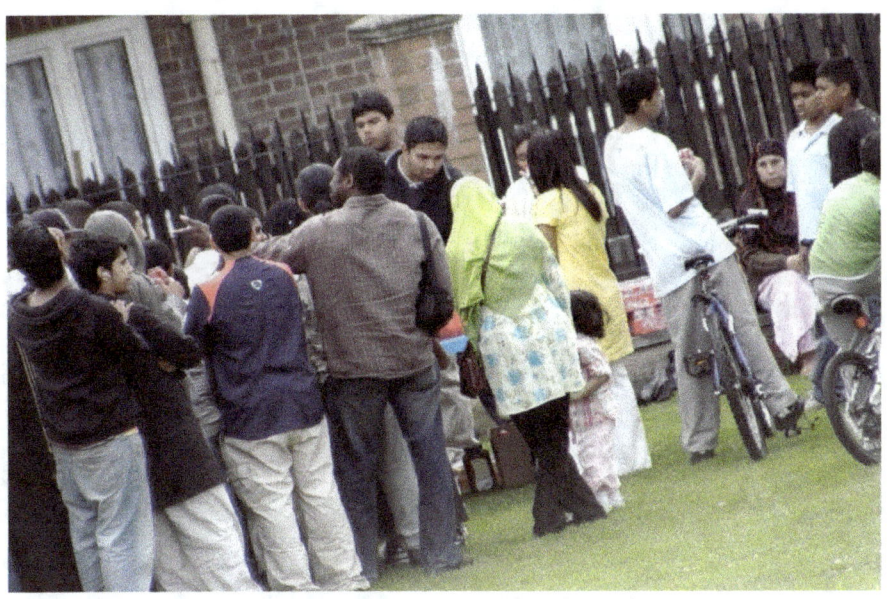

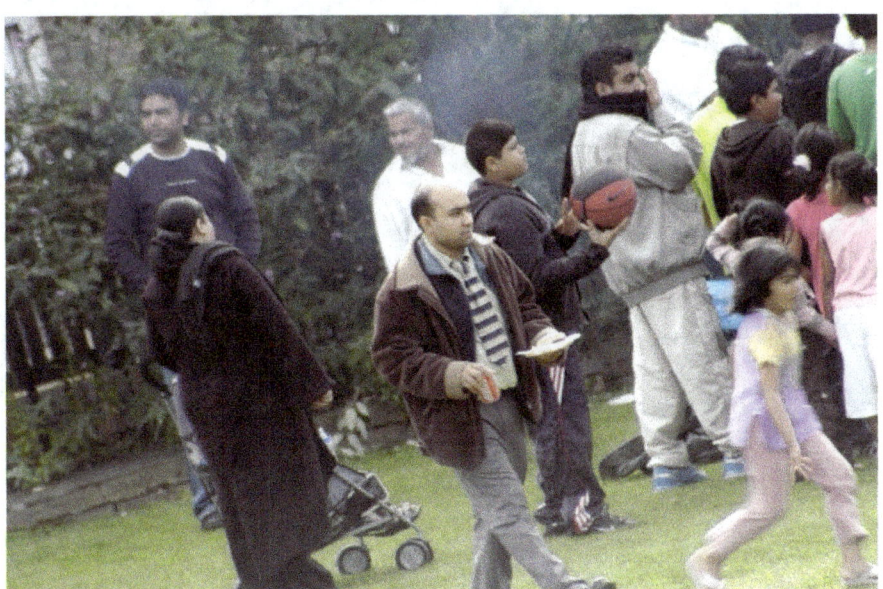

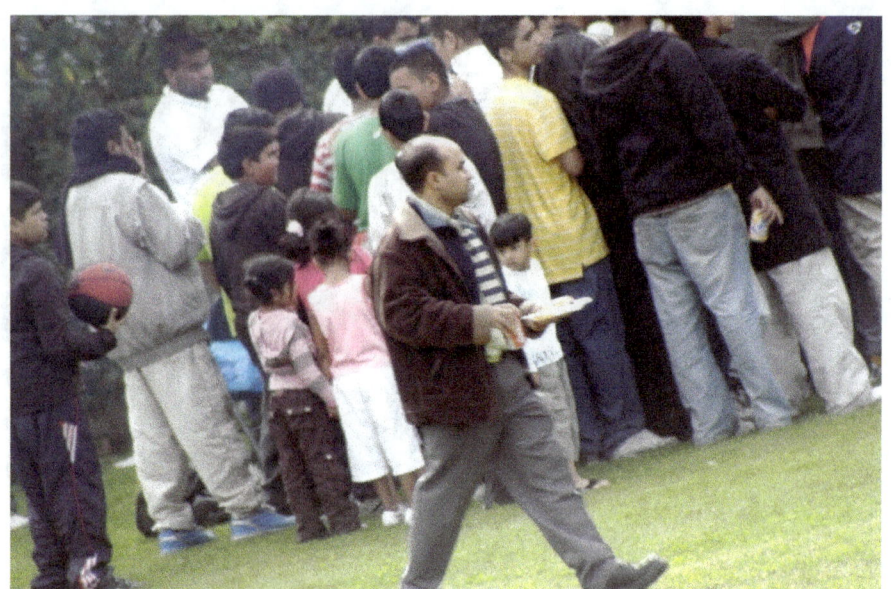

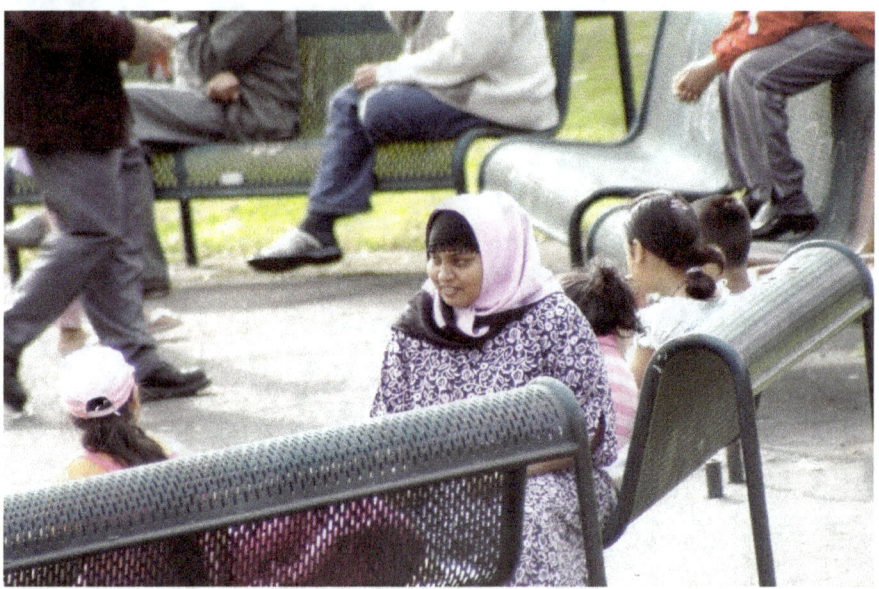

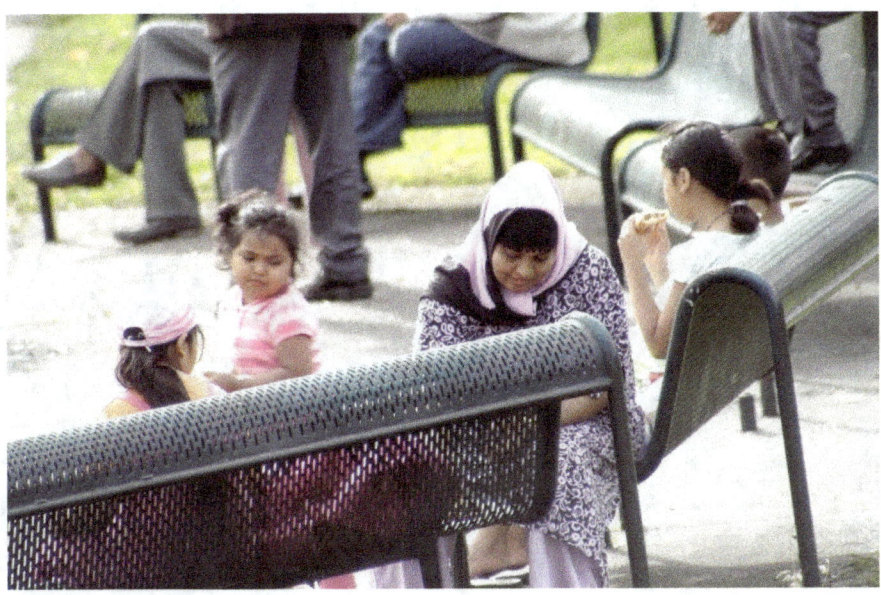

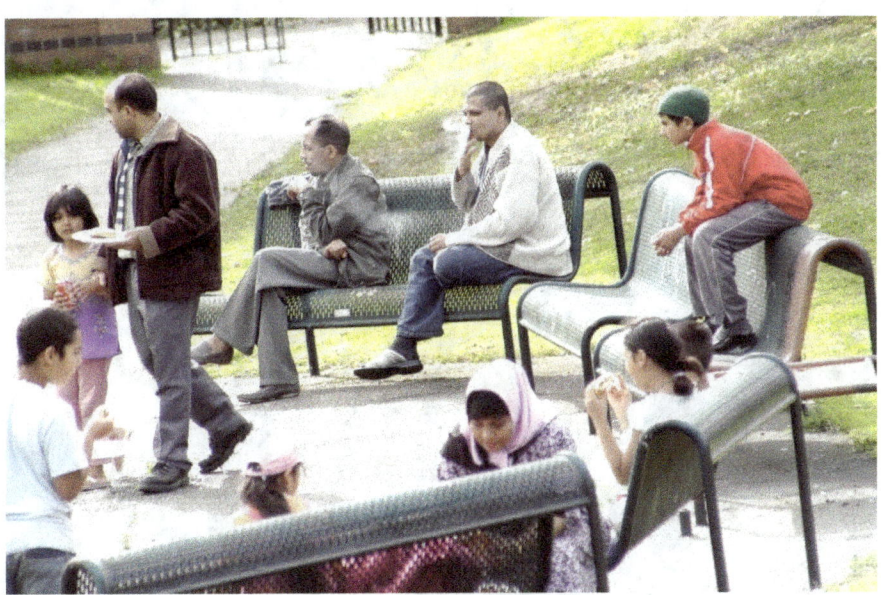

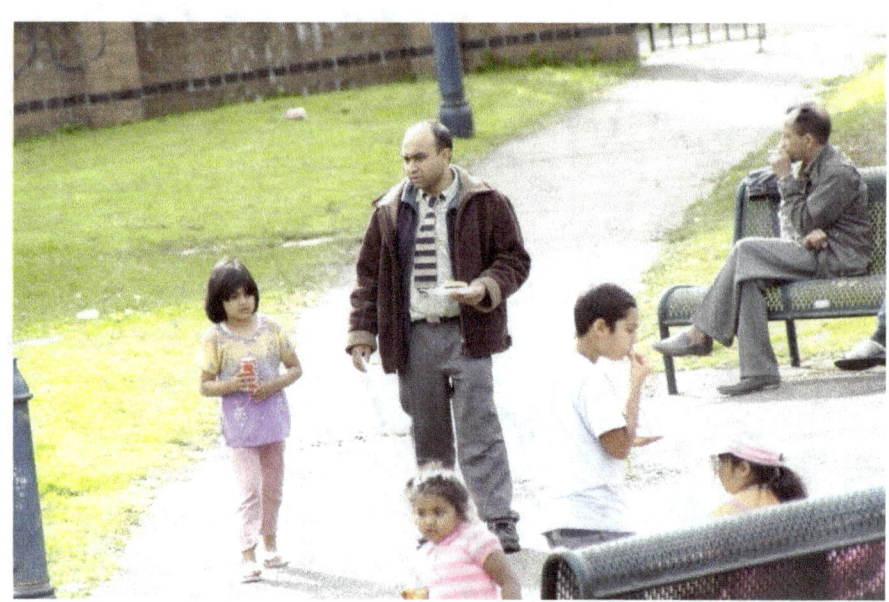

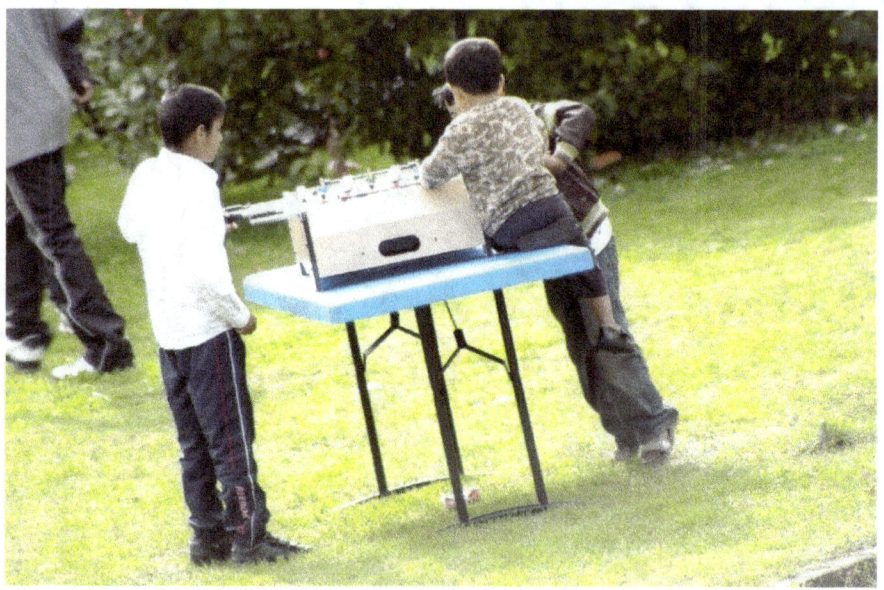

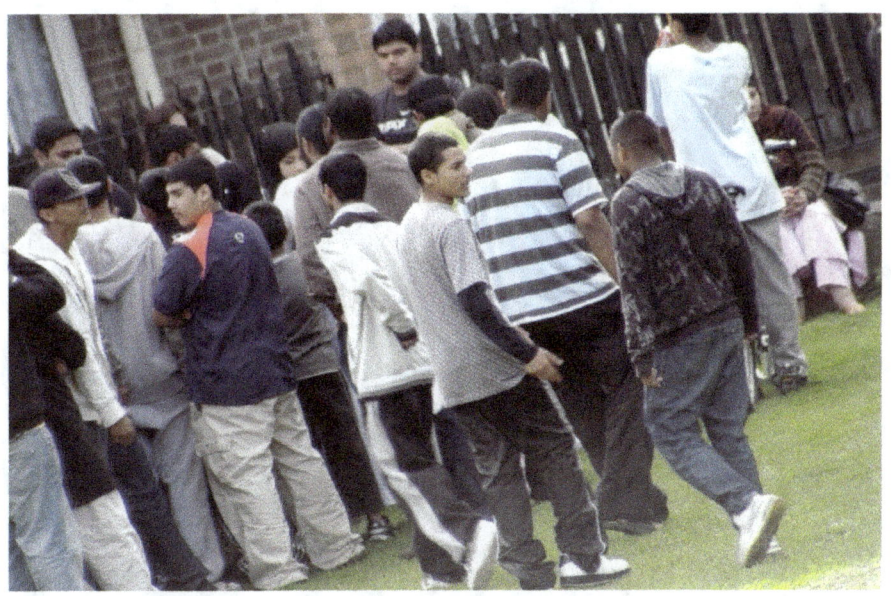

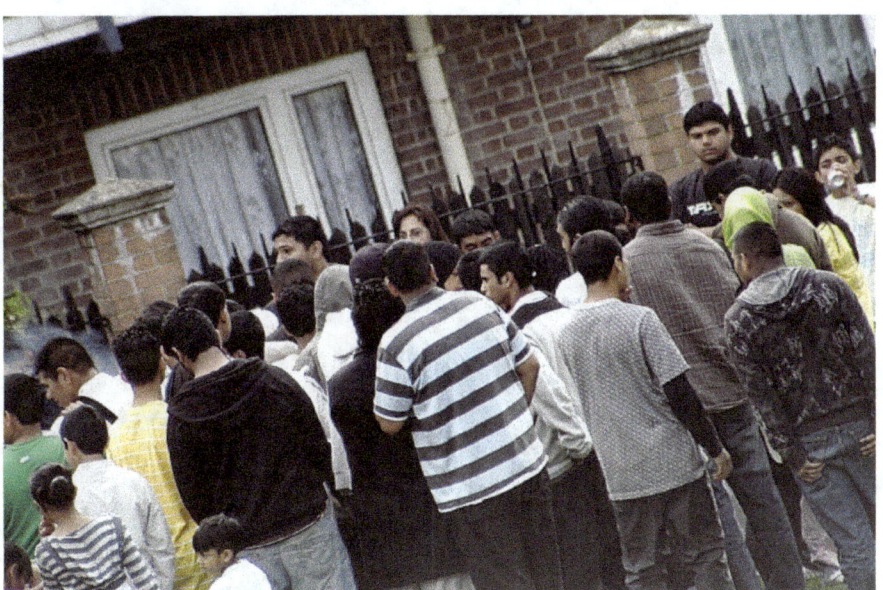

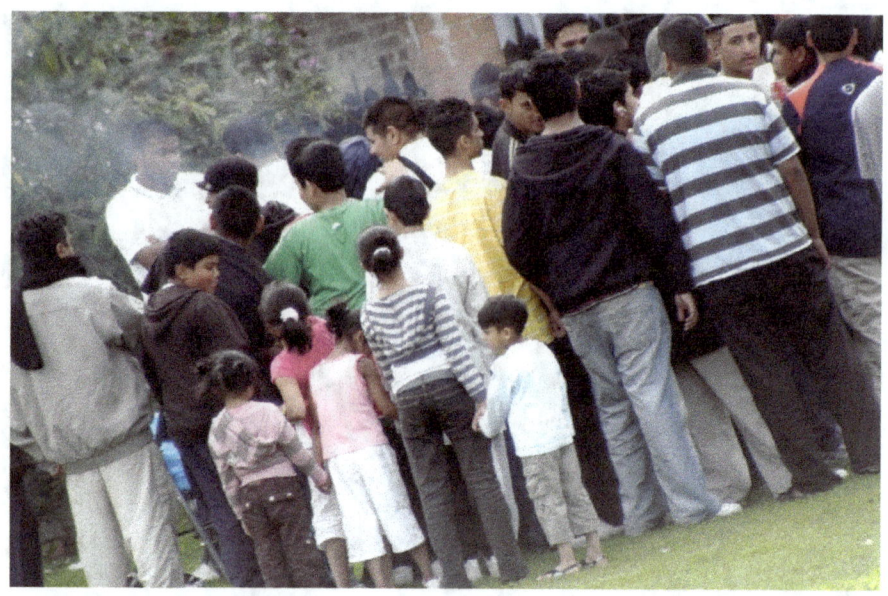

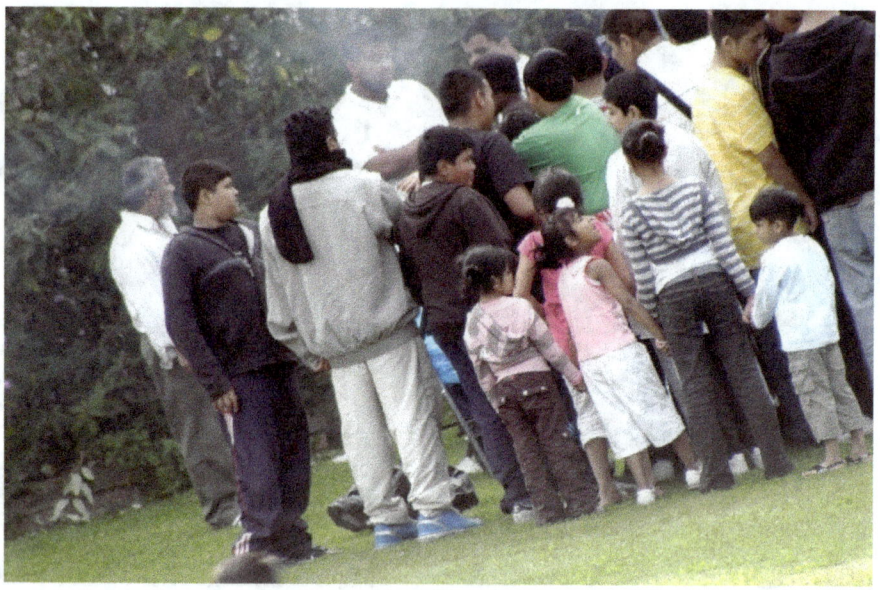

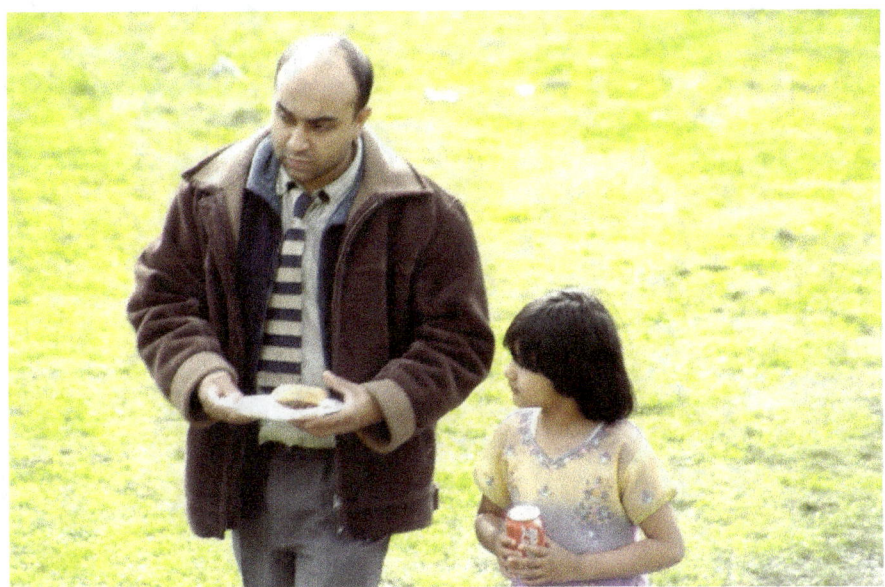

Parents out with their children and enjoying the food served on the day.

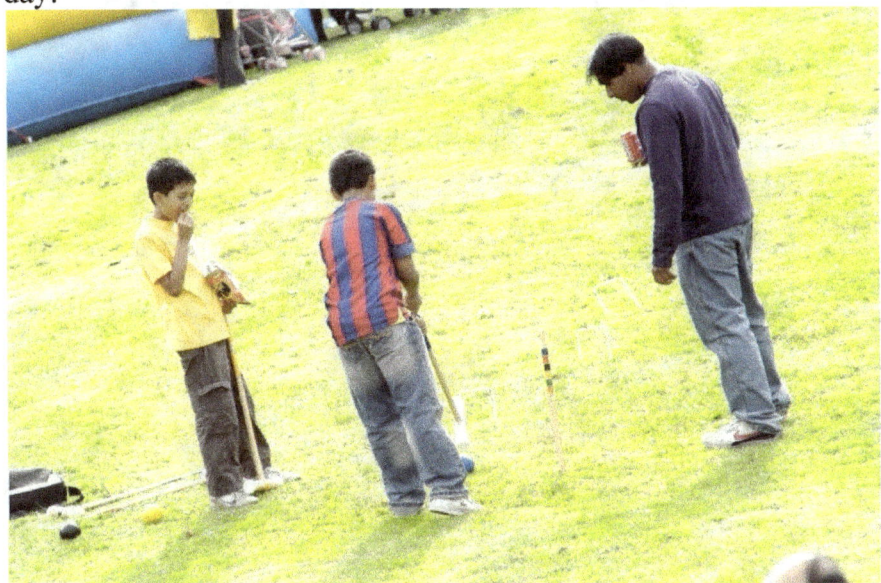

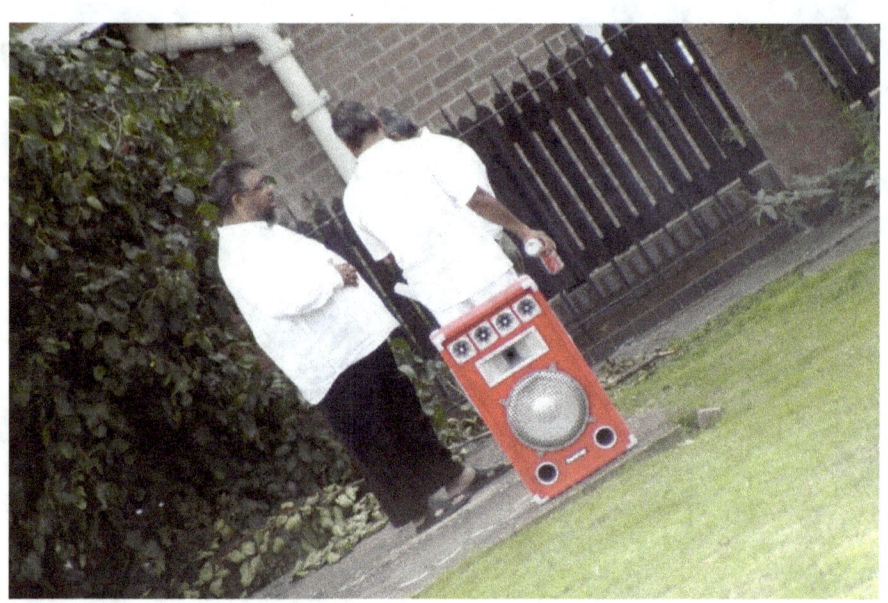

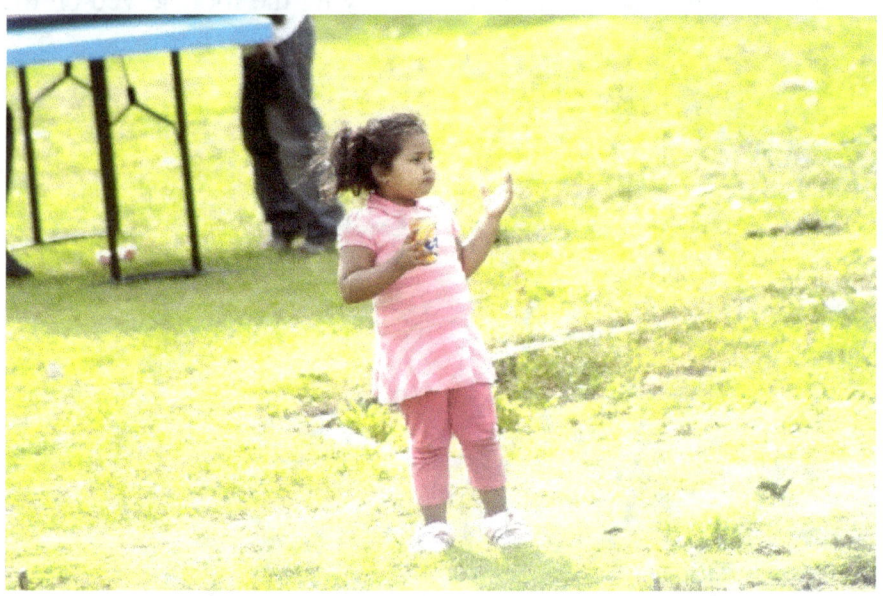

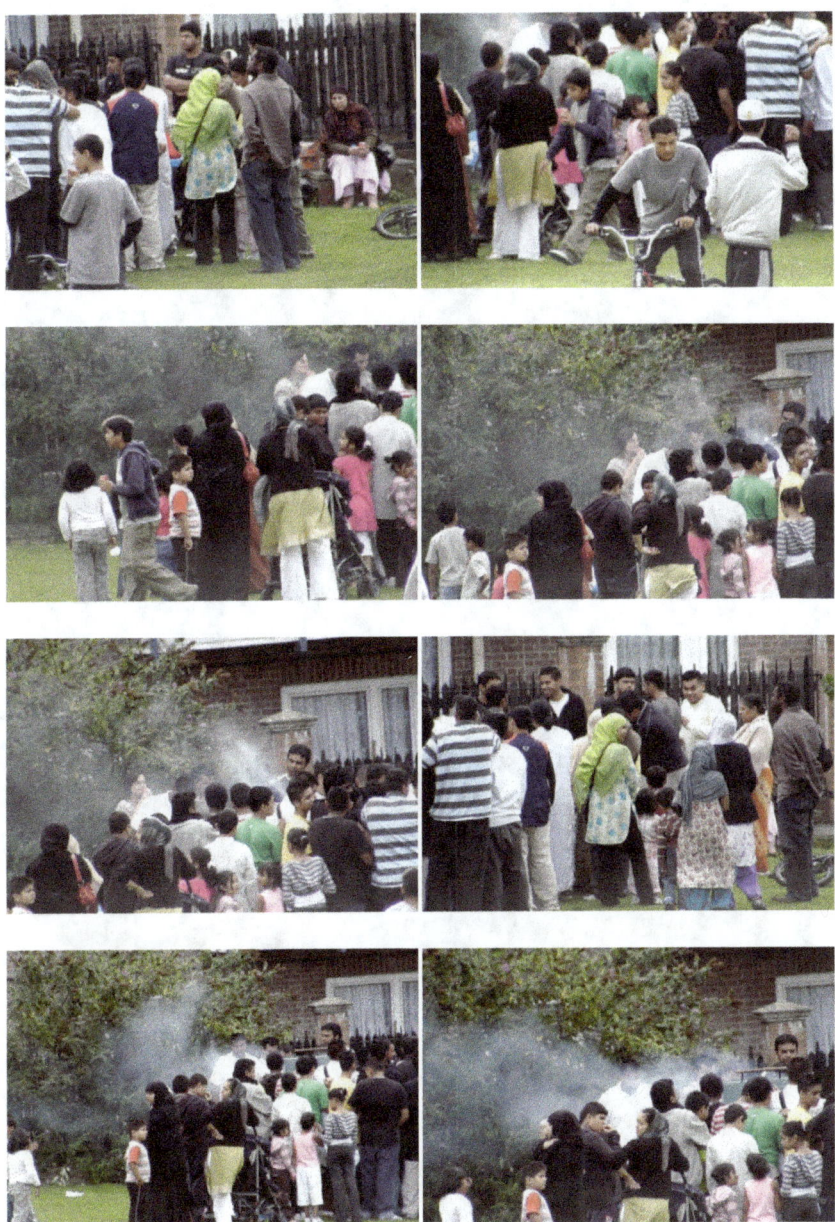

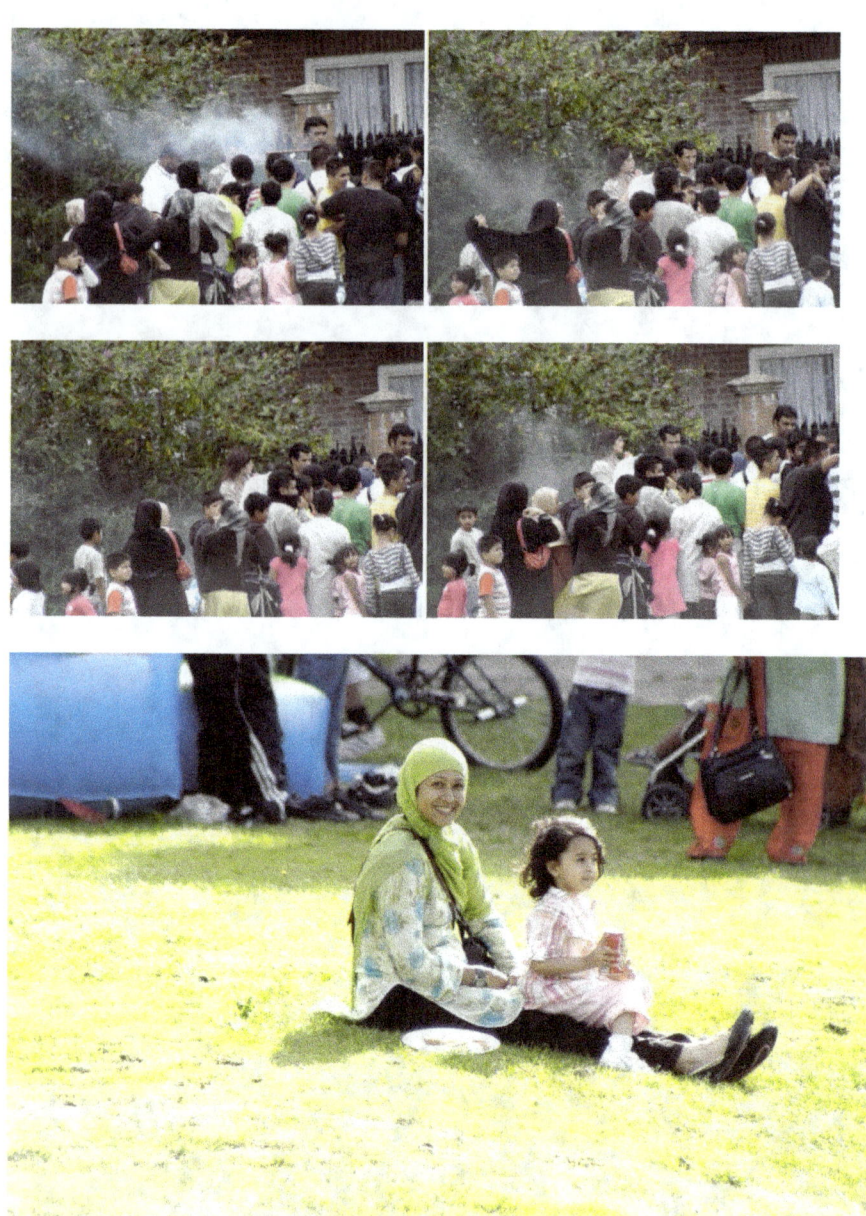

Mother and daughter savouring the BBQ

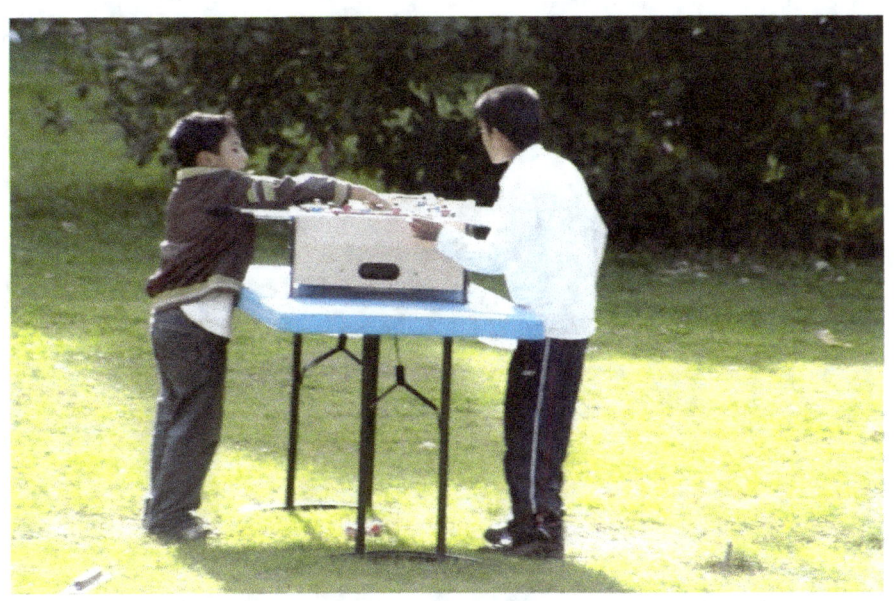

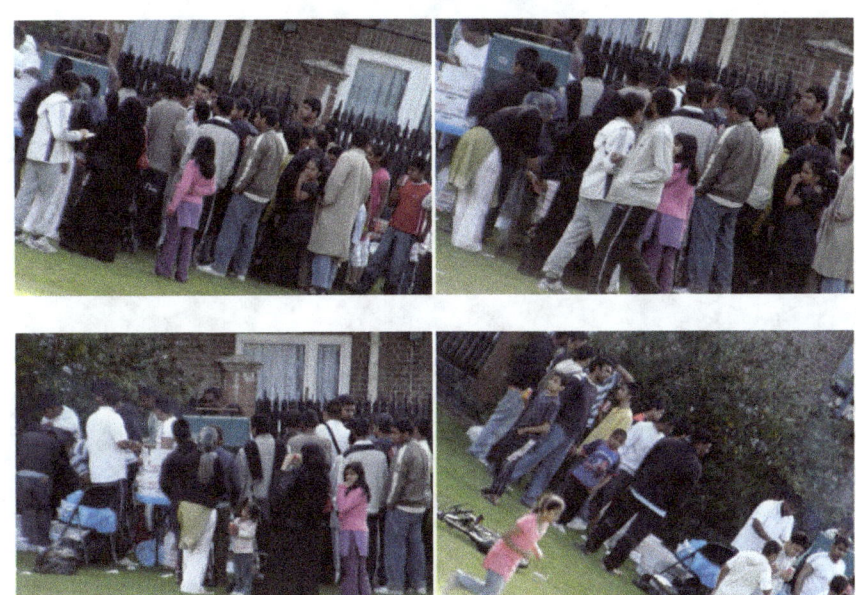

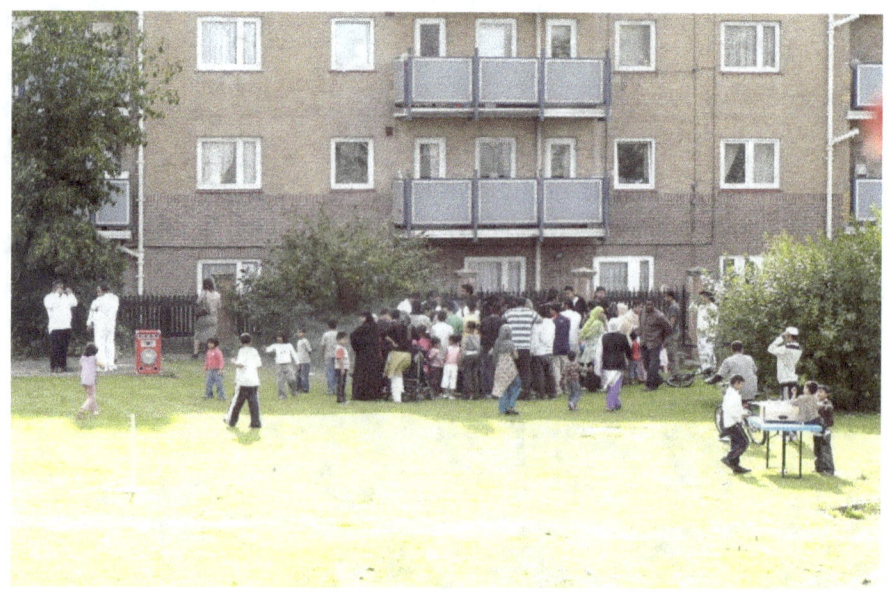

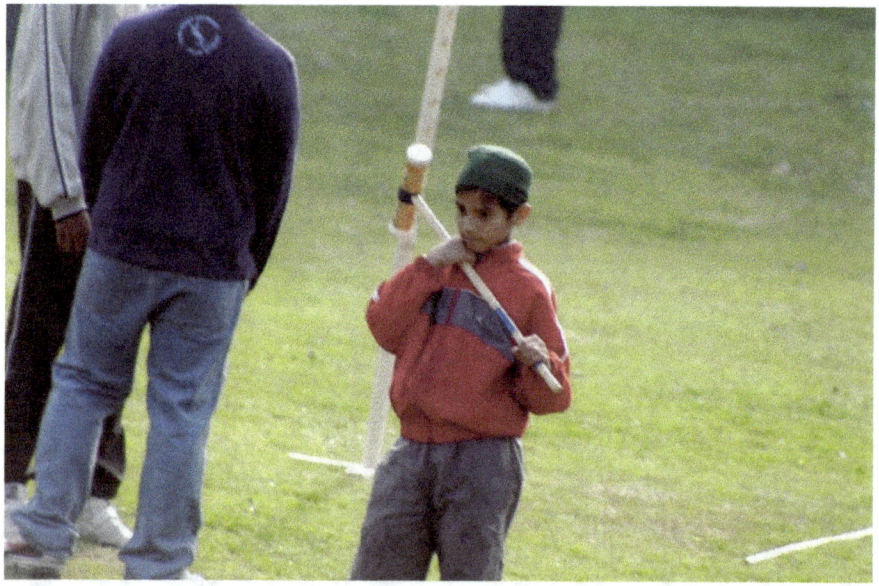

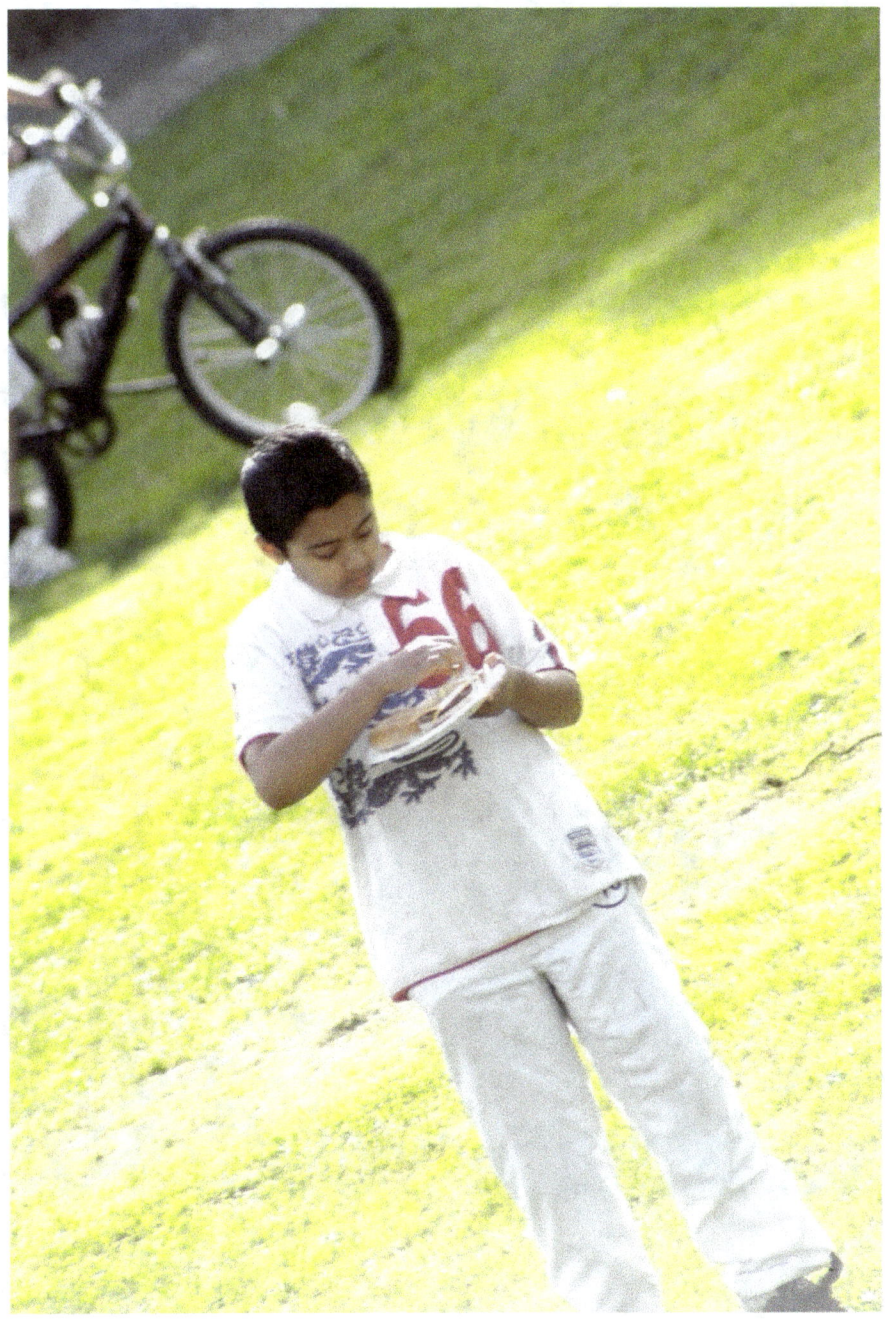

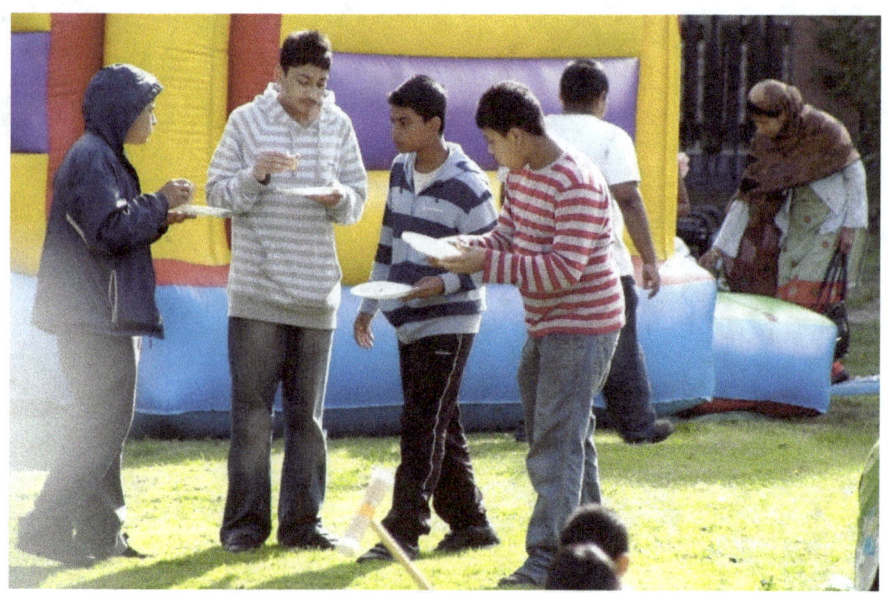

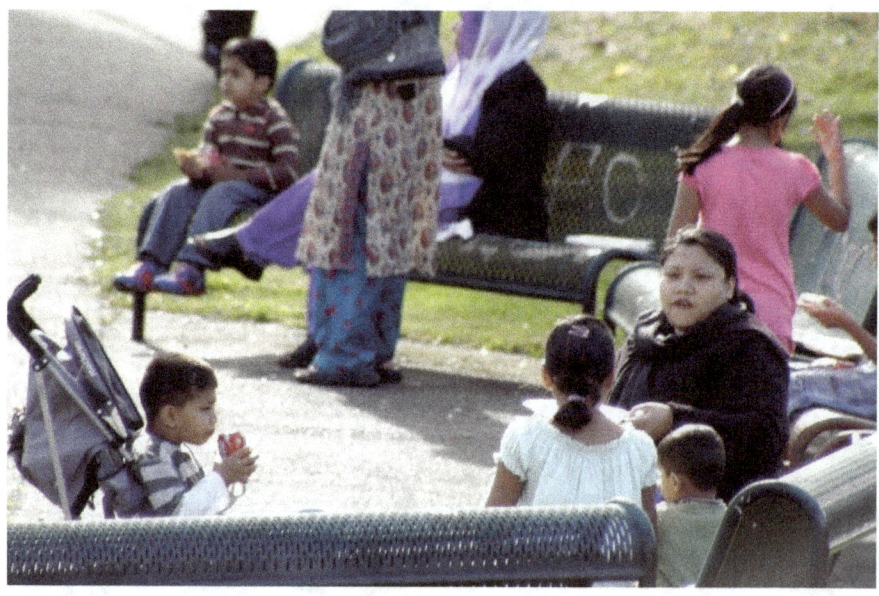

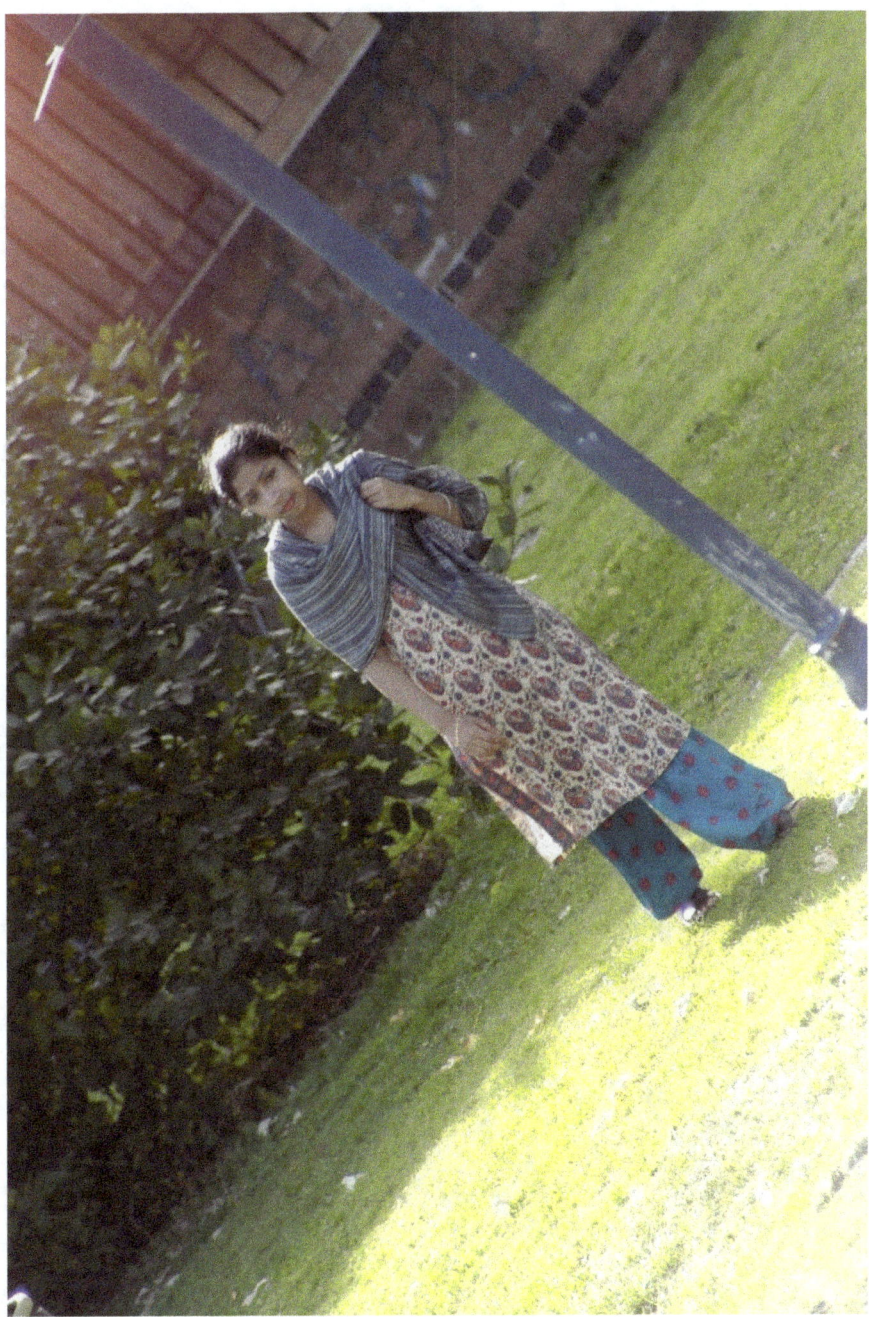

Keeping an eye on her child

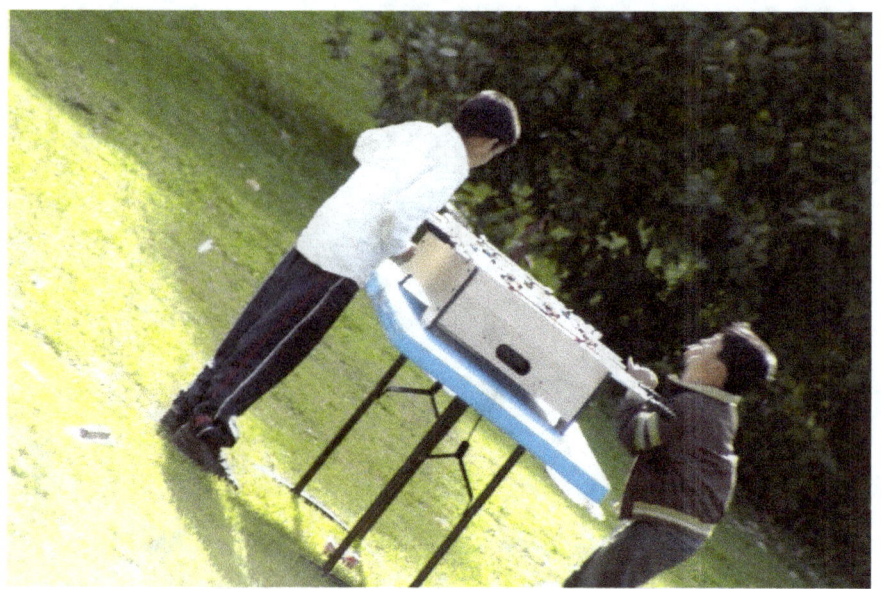

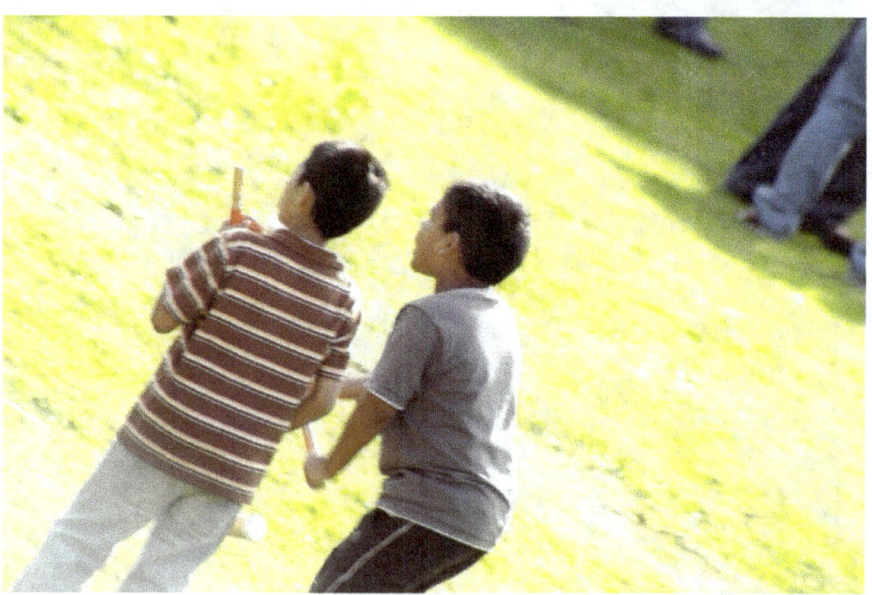

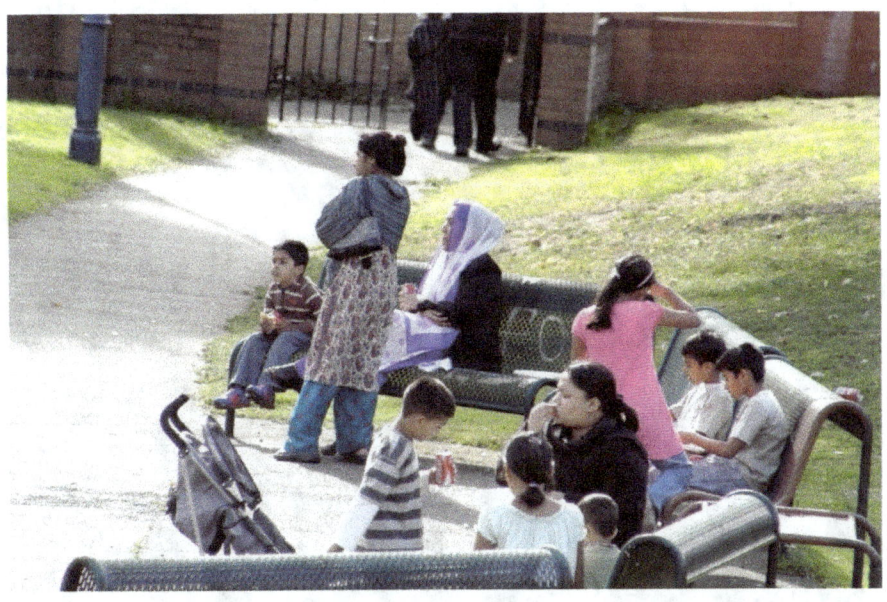

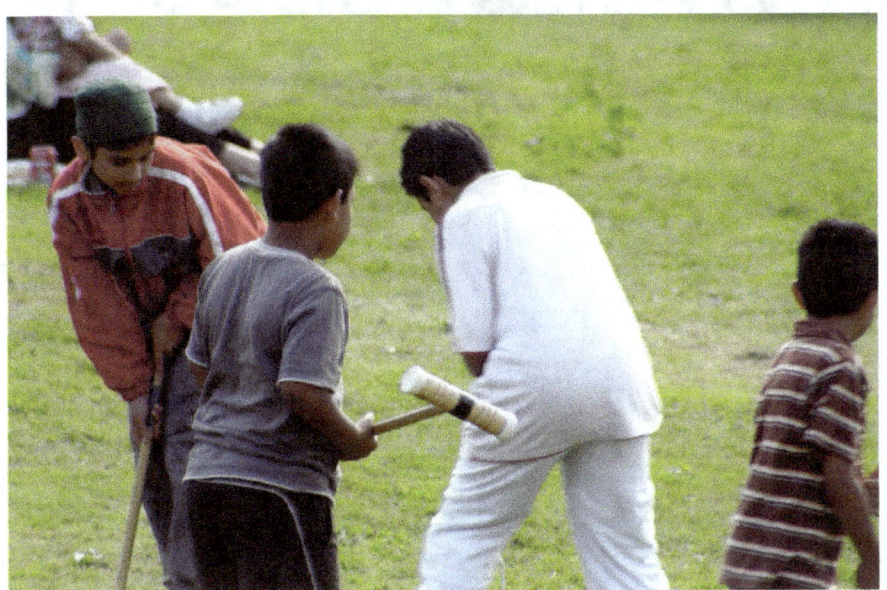

Mayar Akash

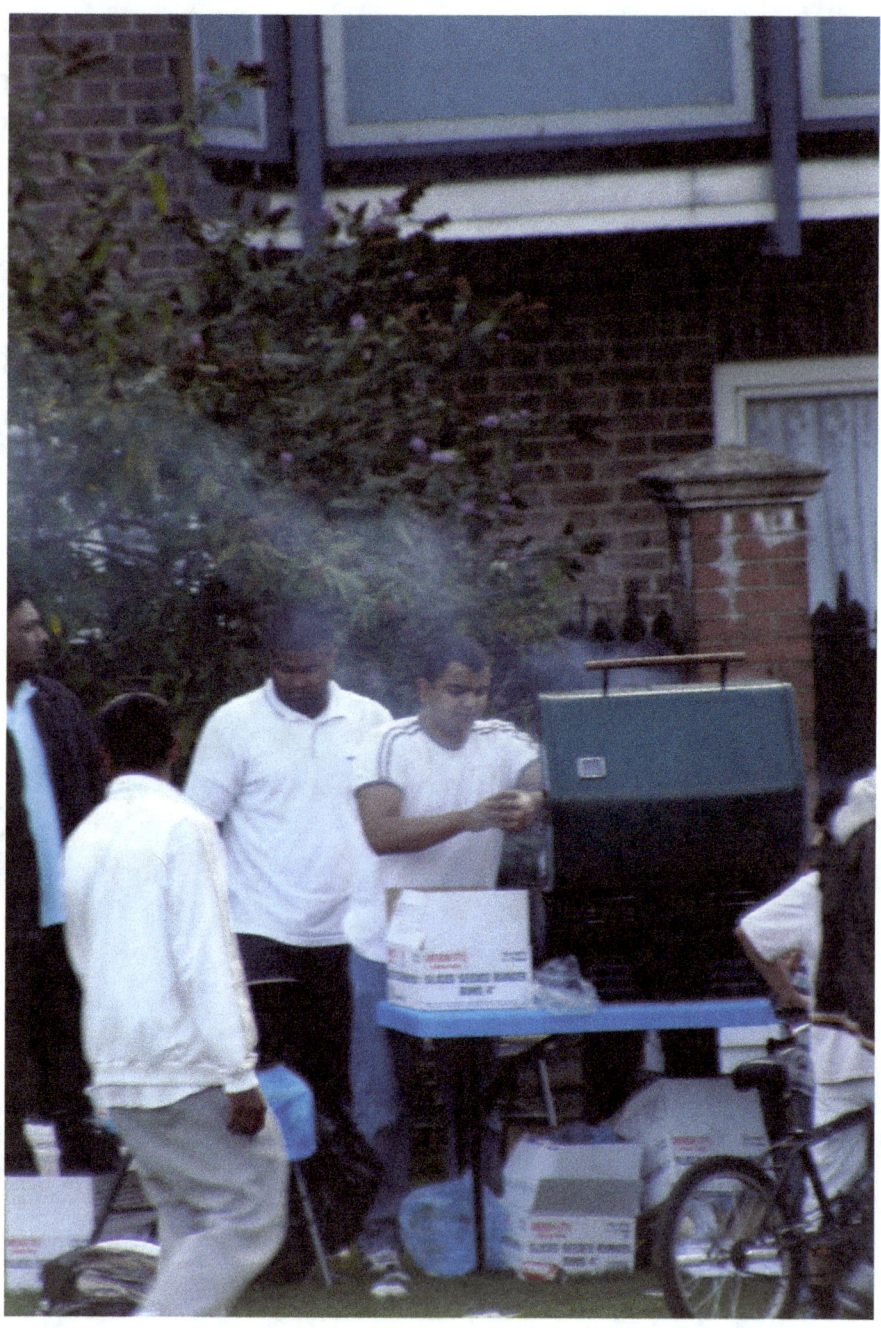

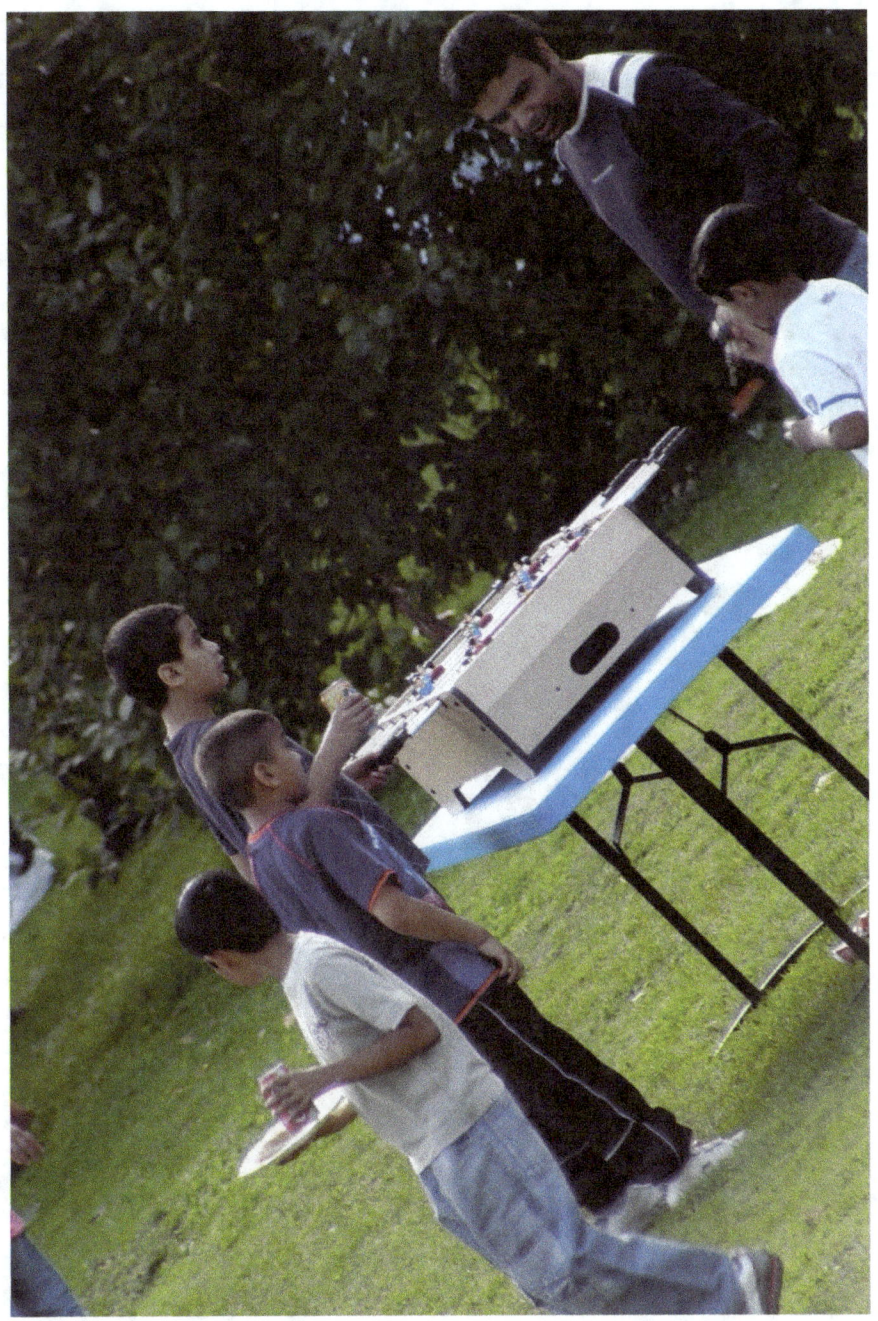

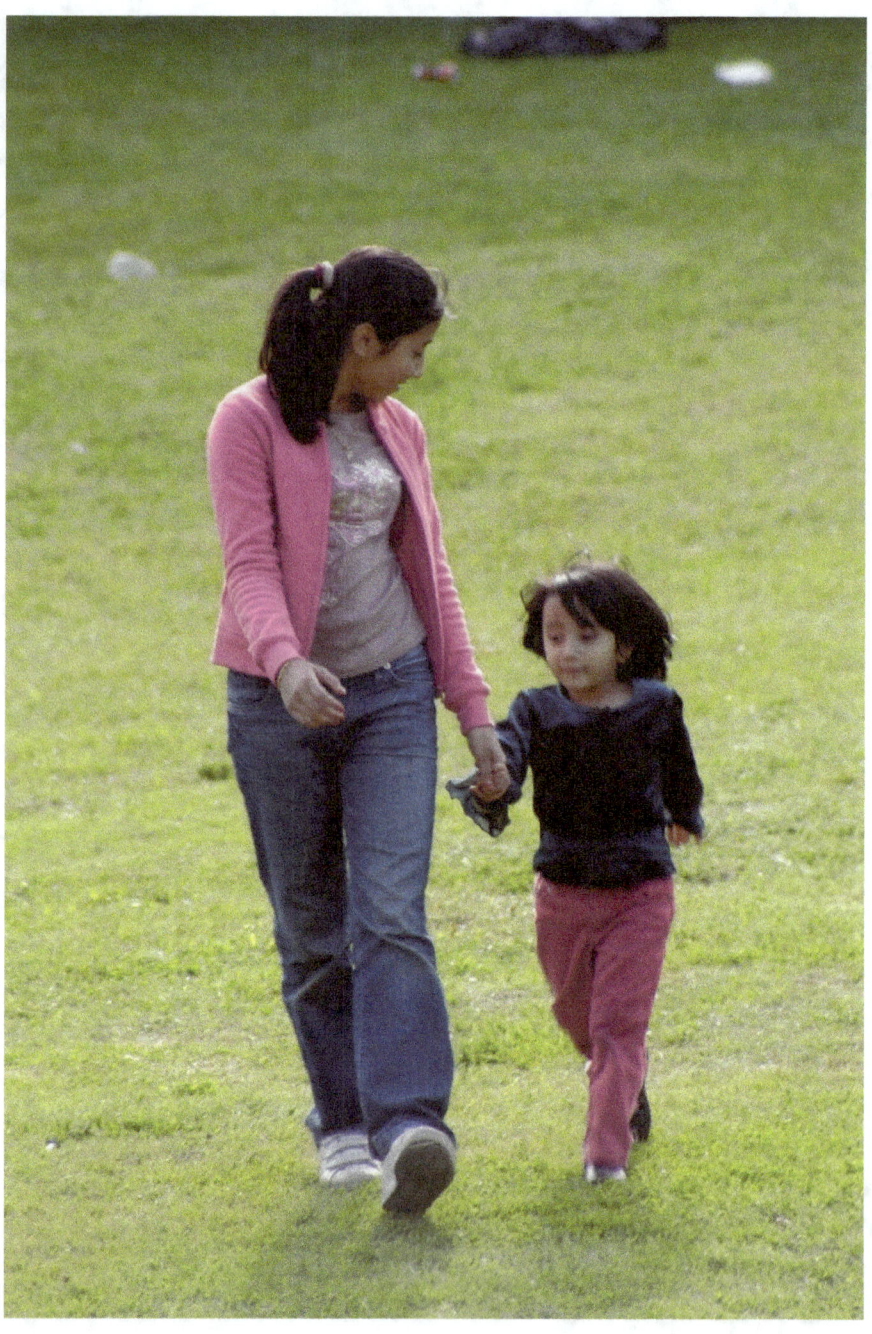

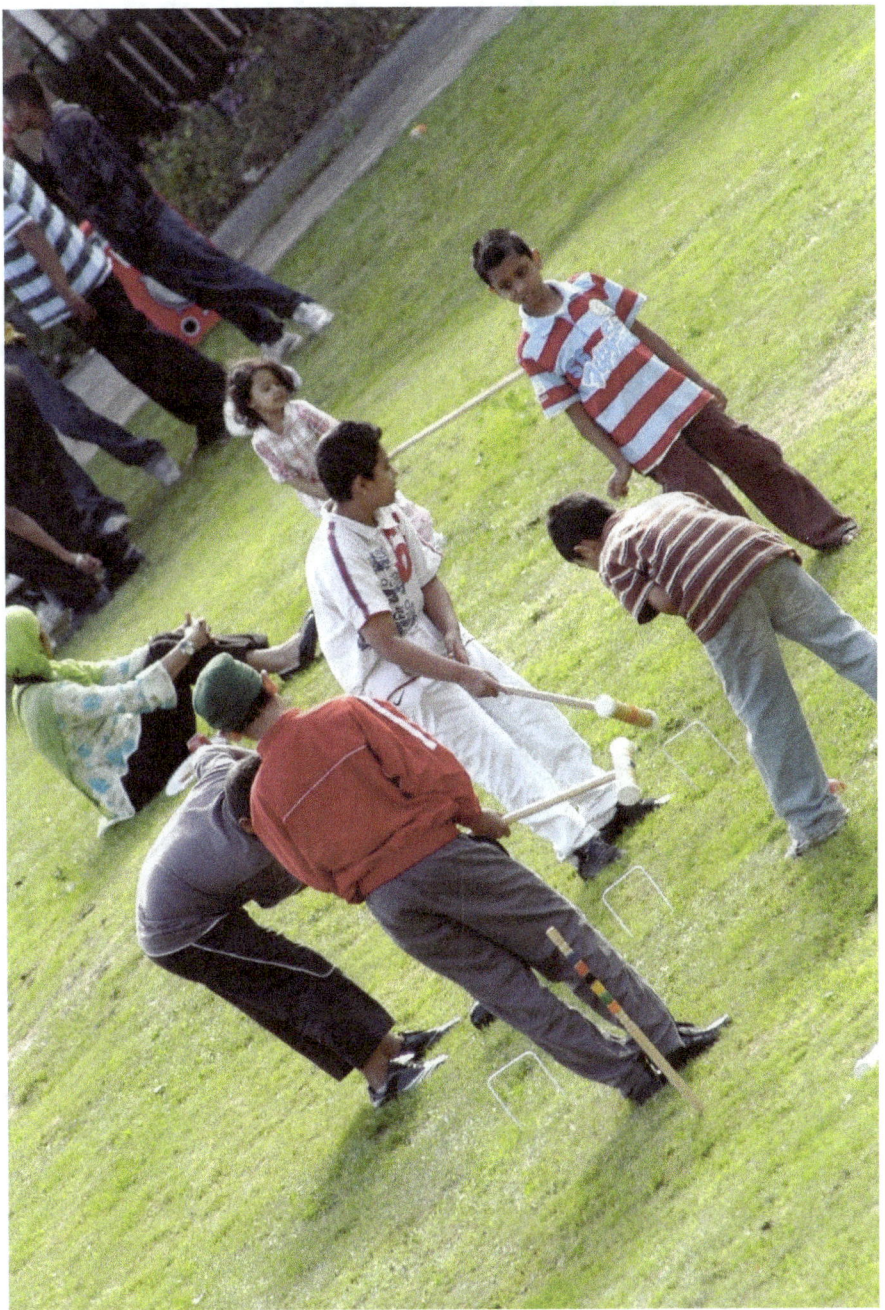

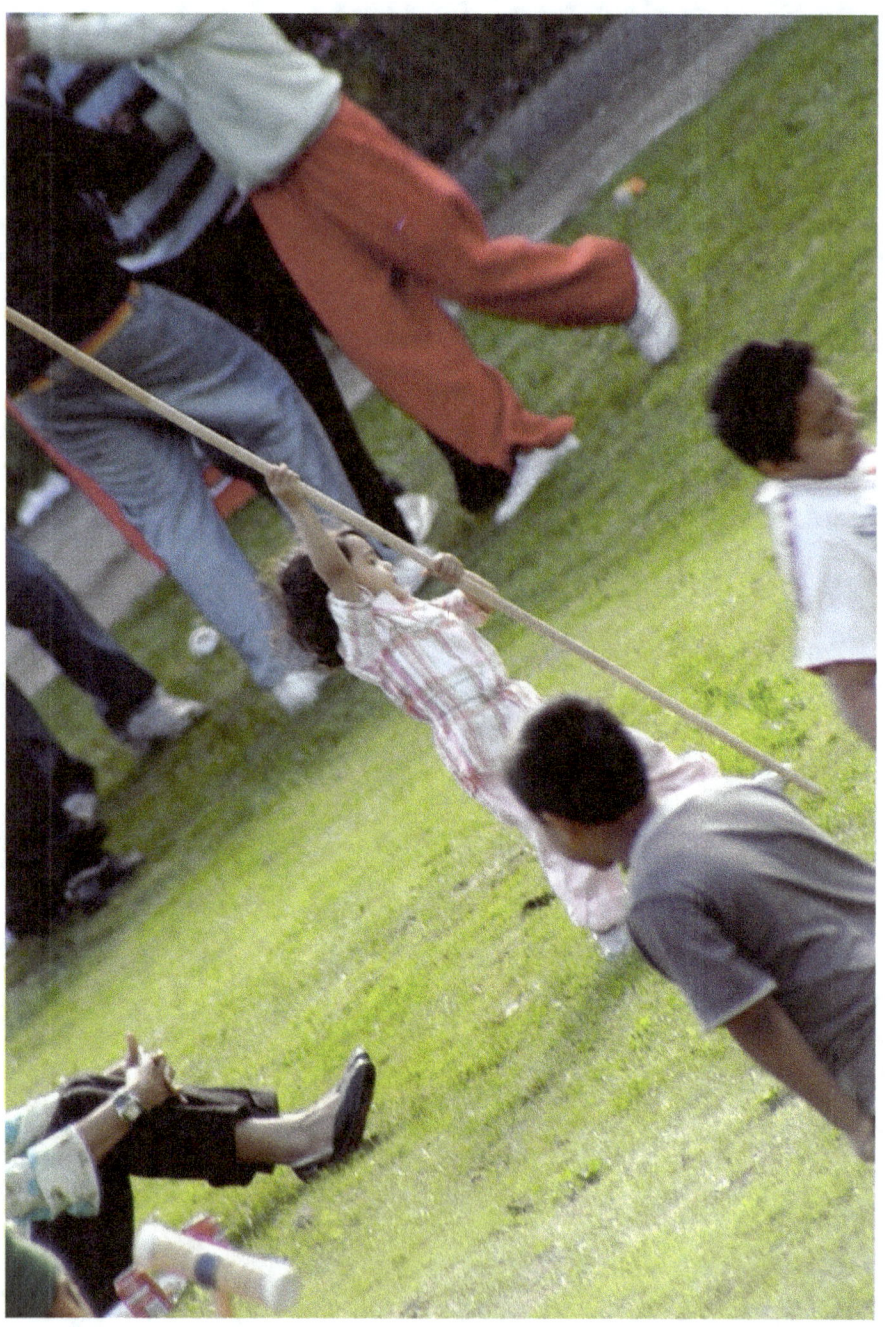

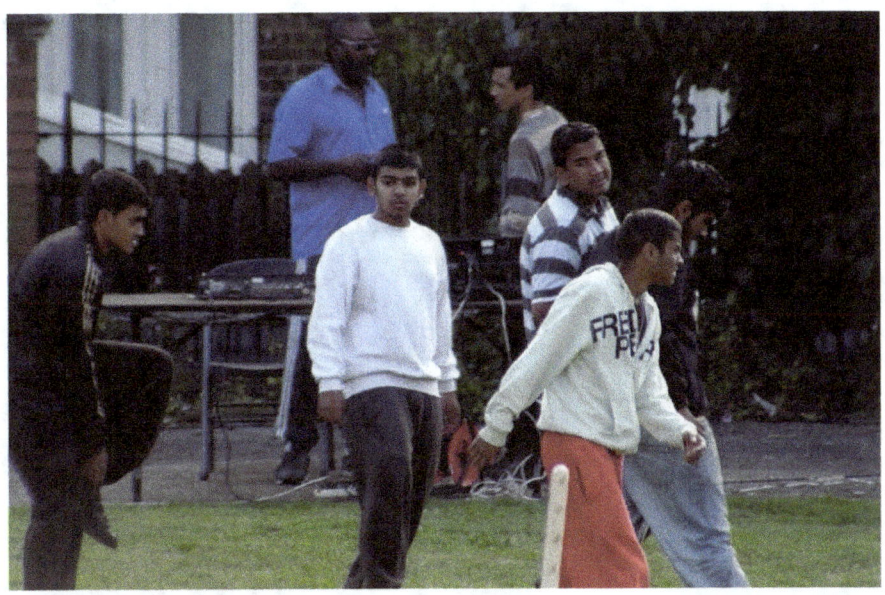

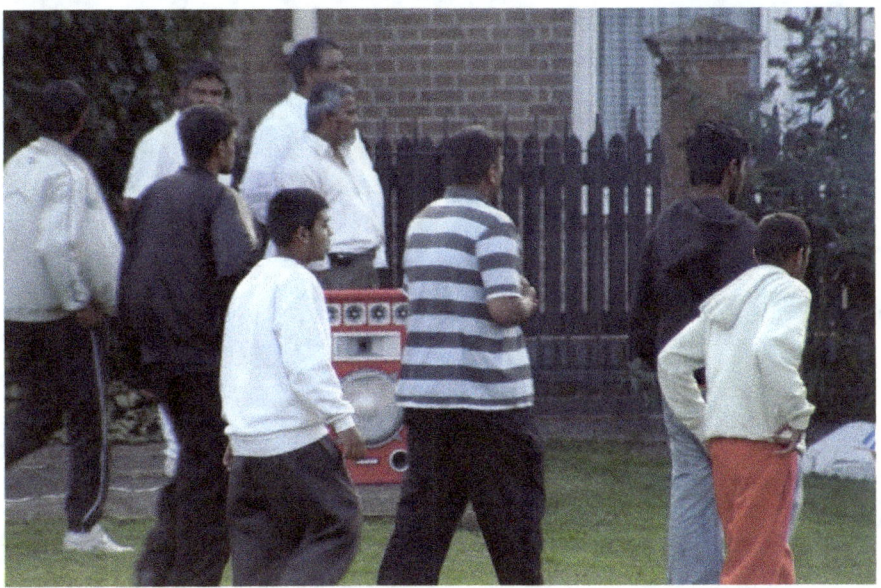

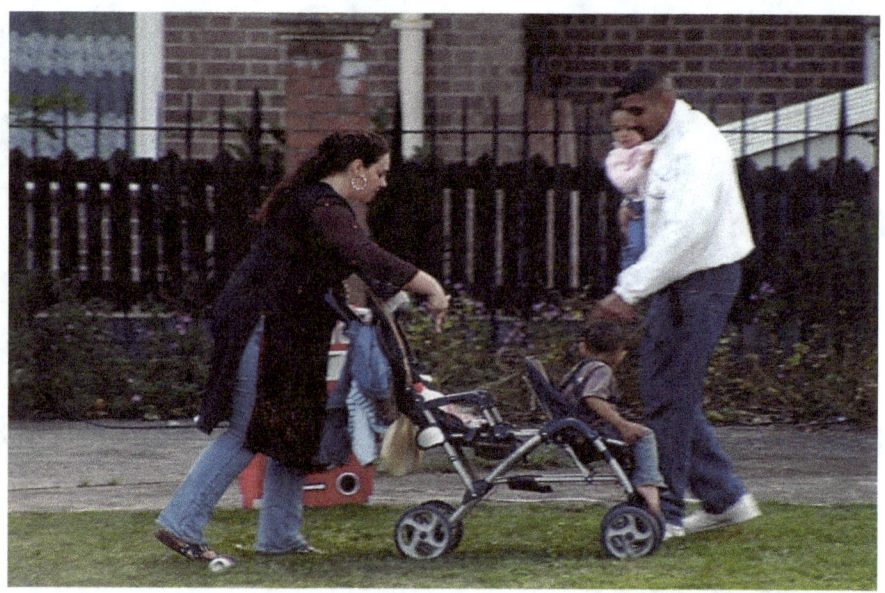

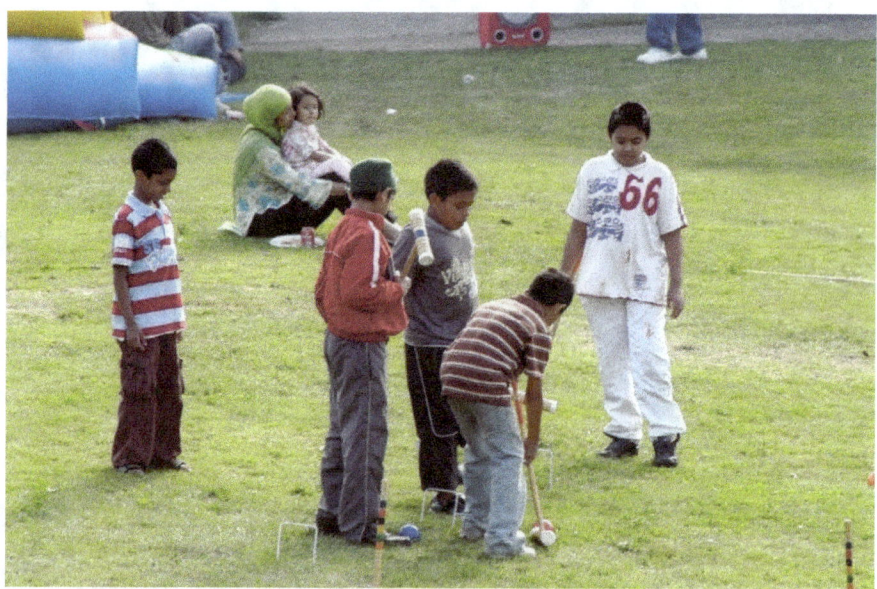

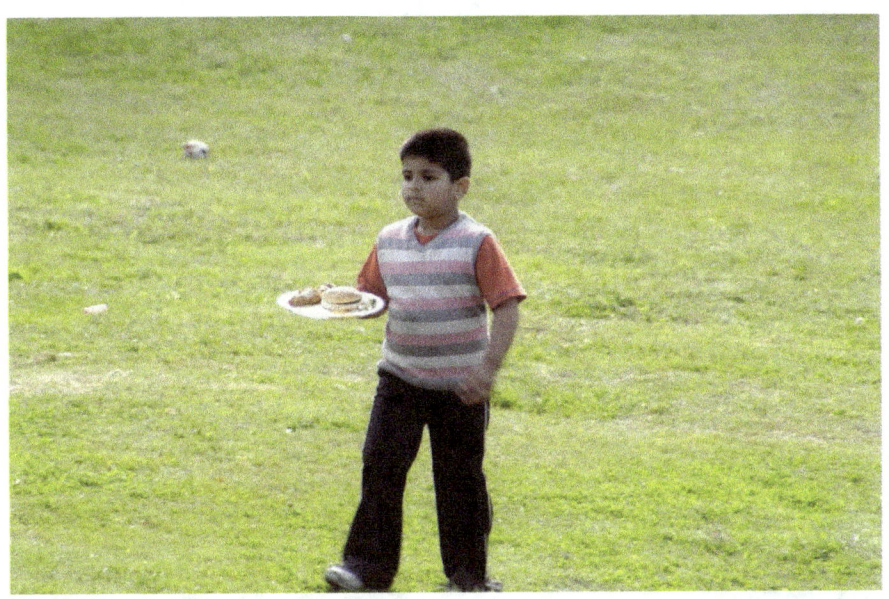

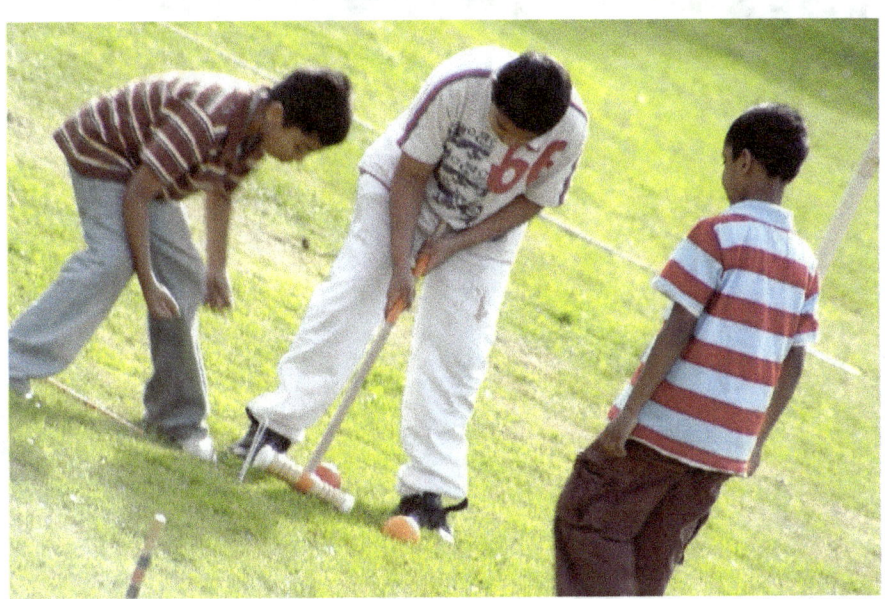

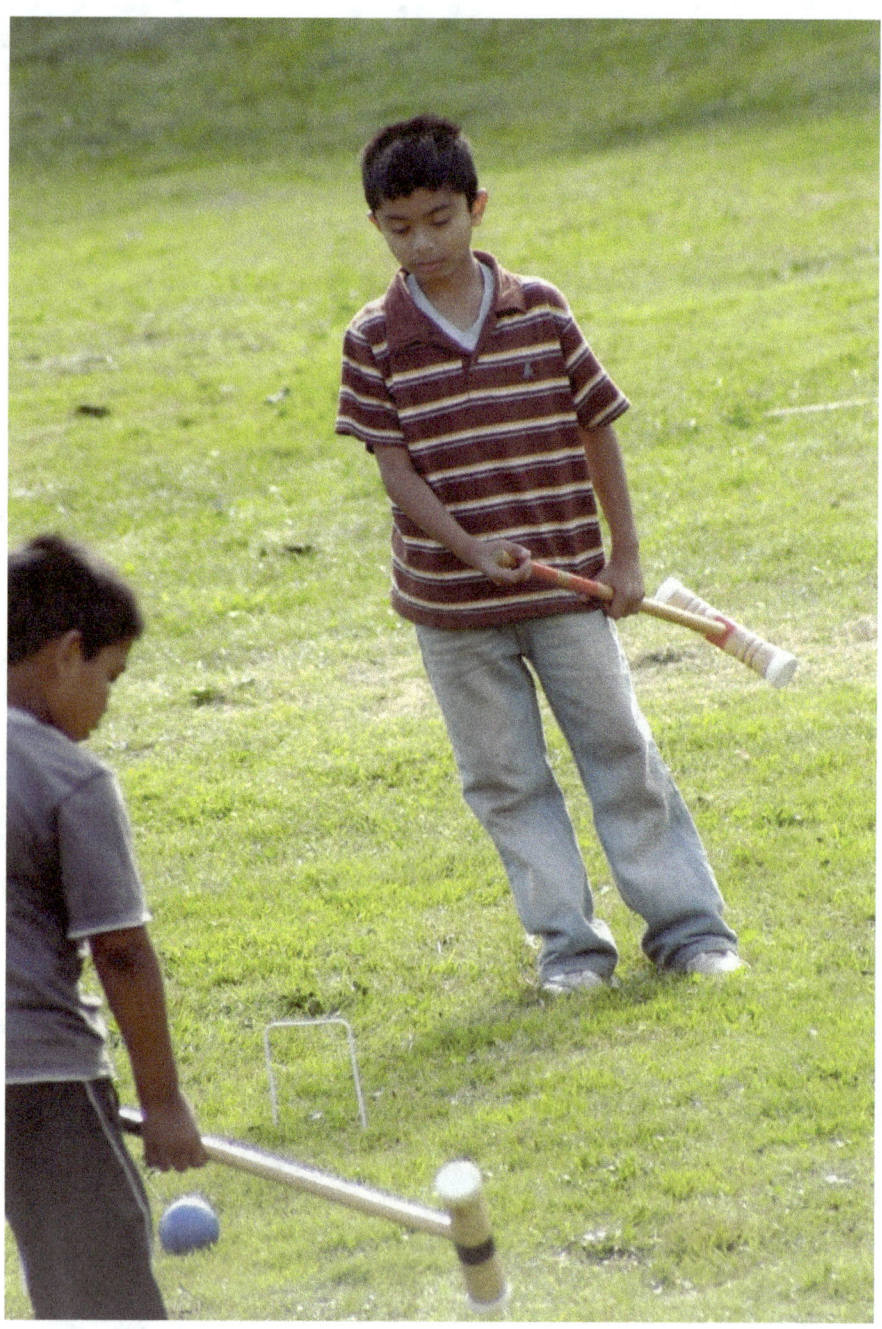

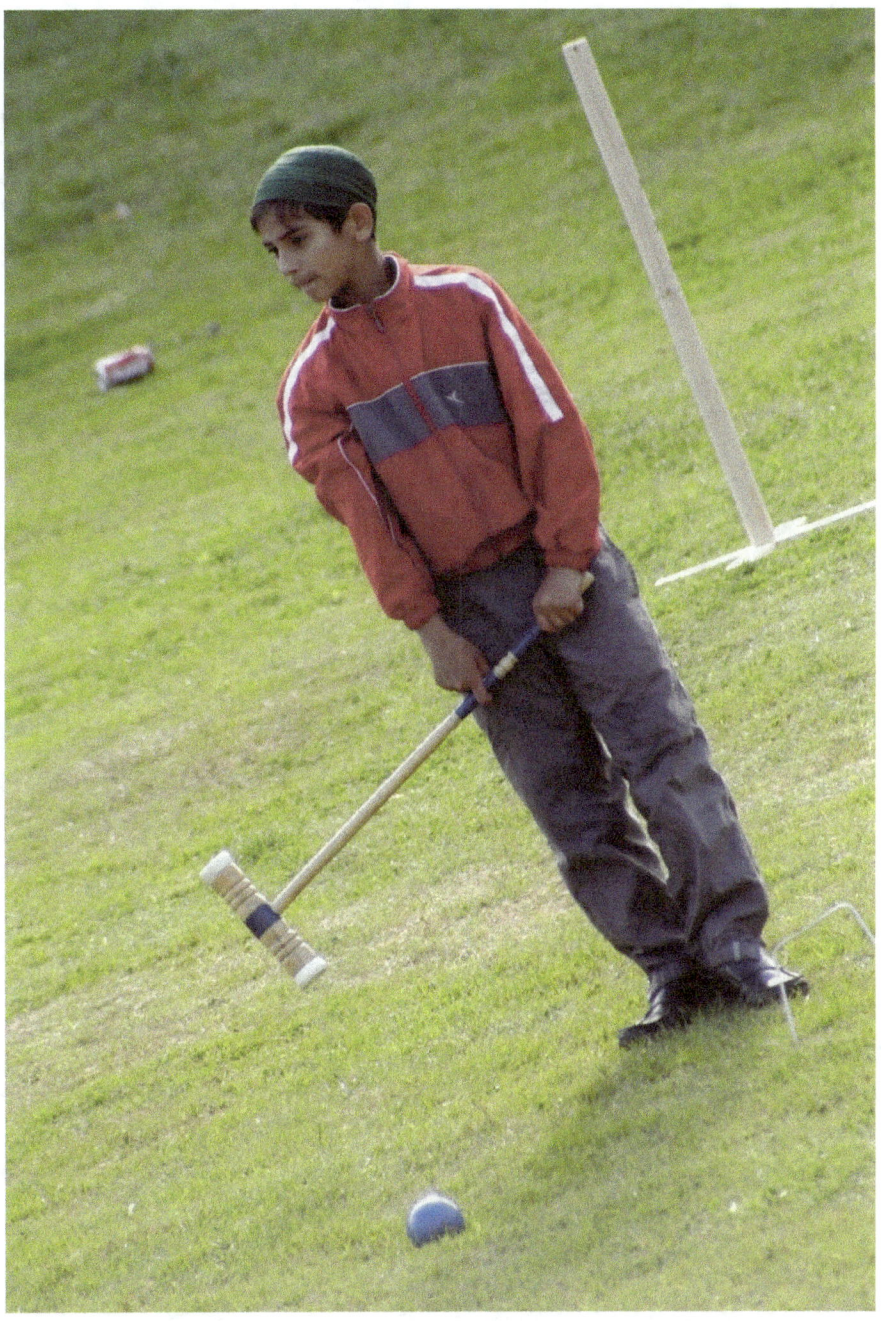

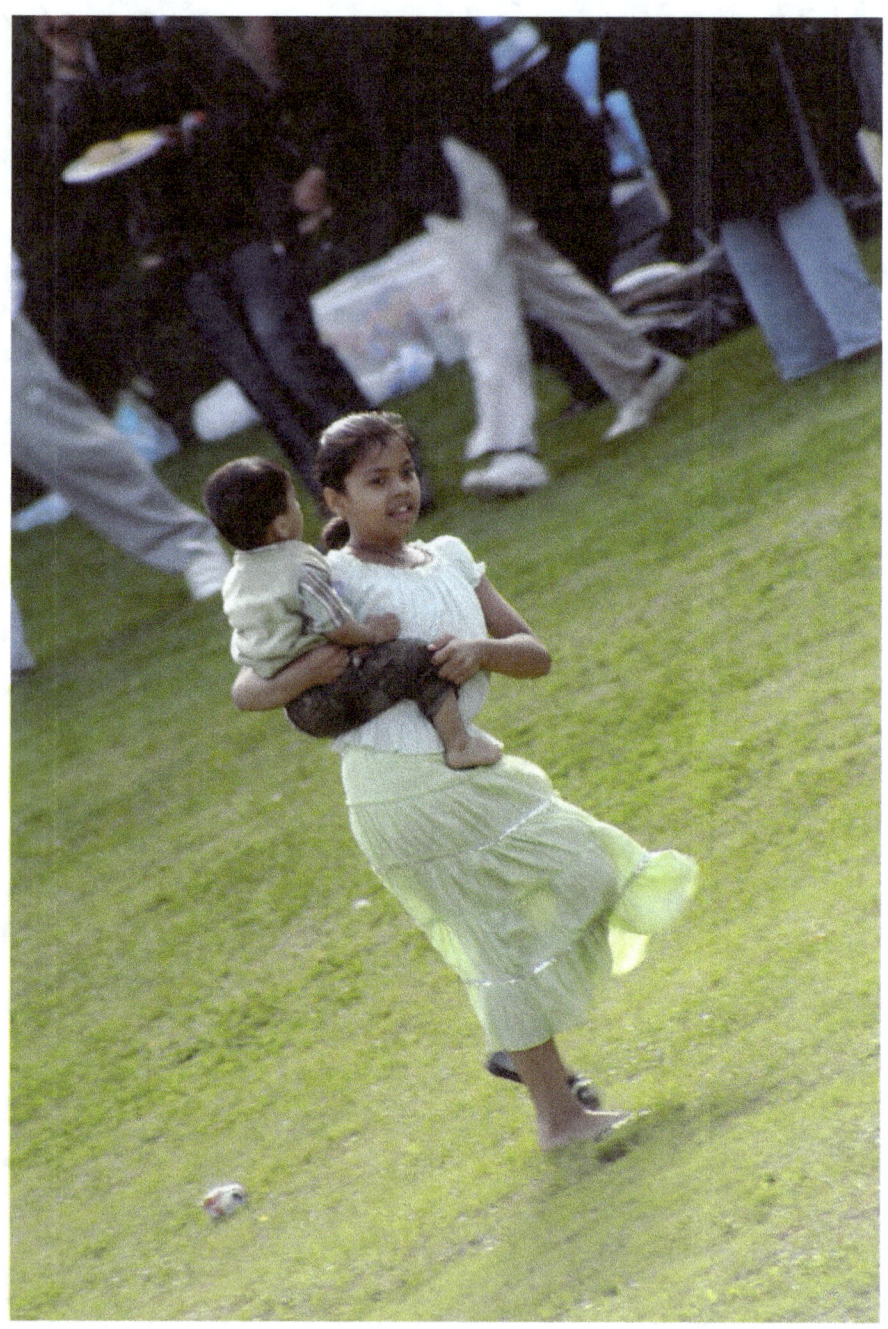

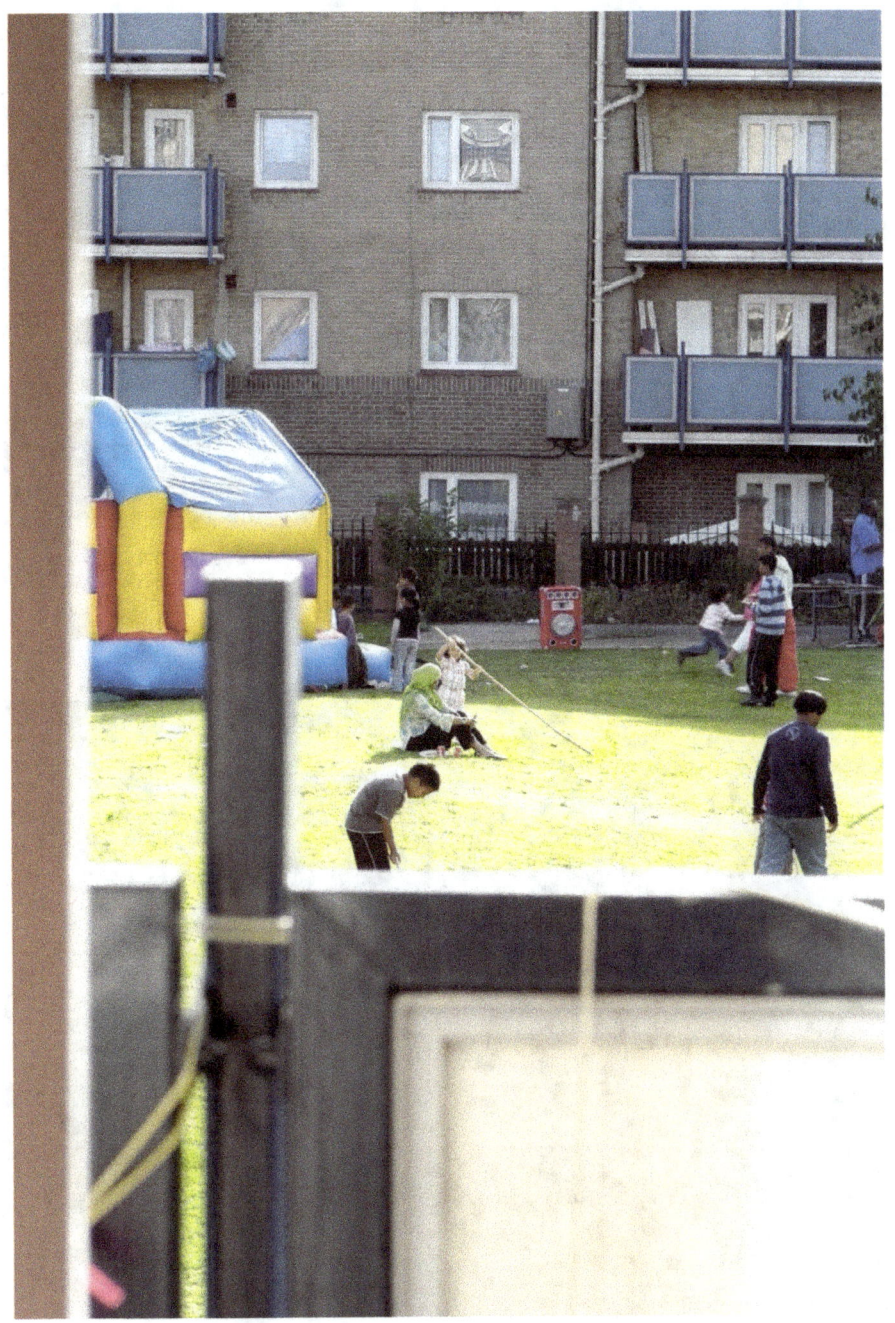

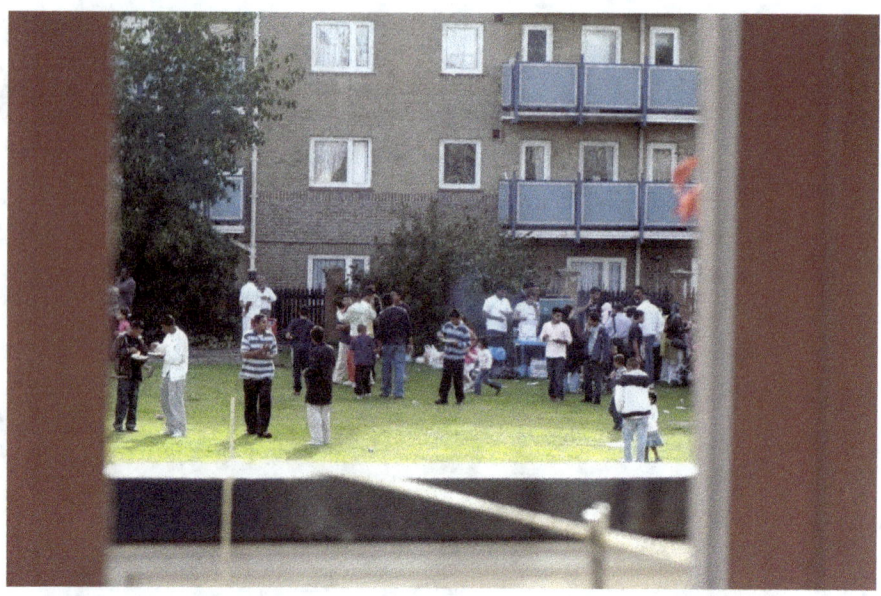

View from the balcony

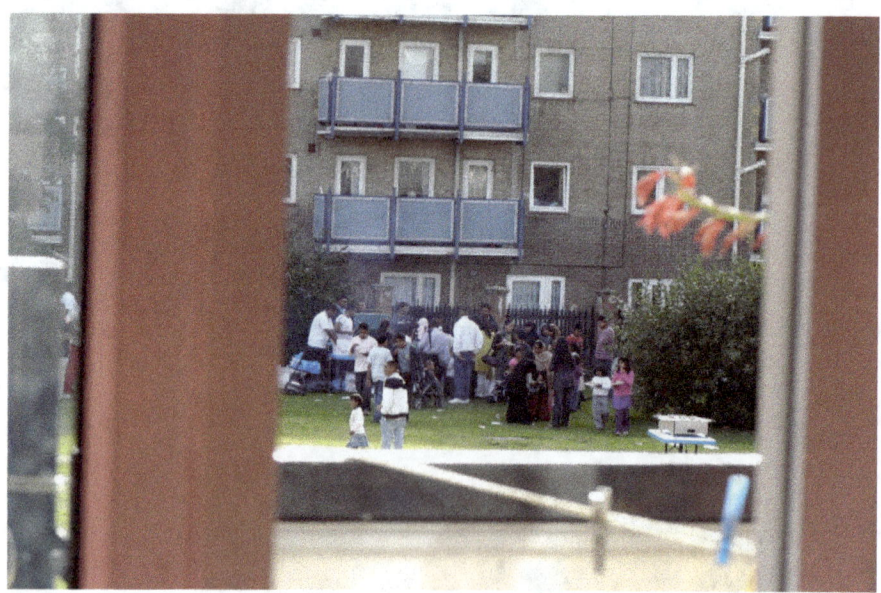

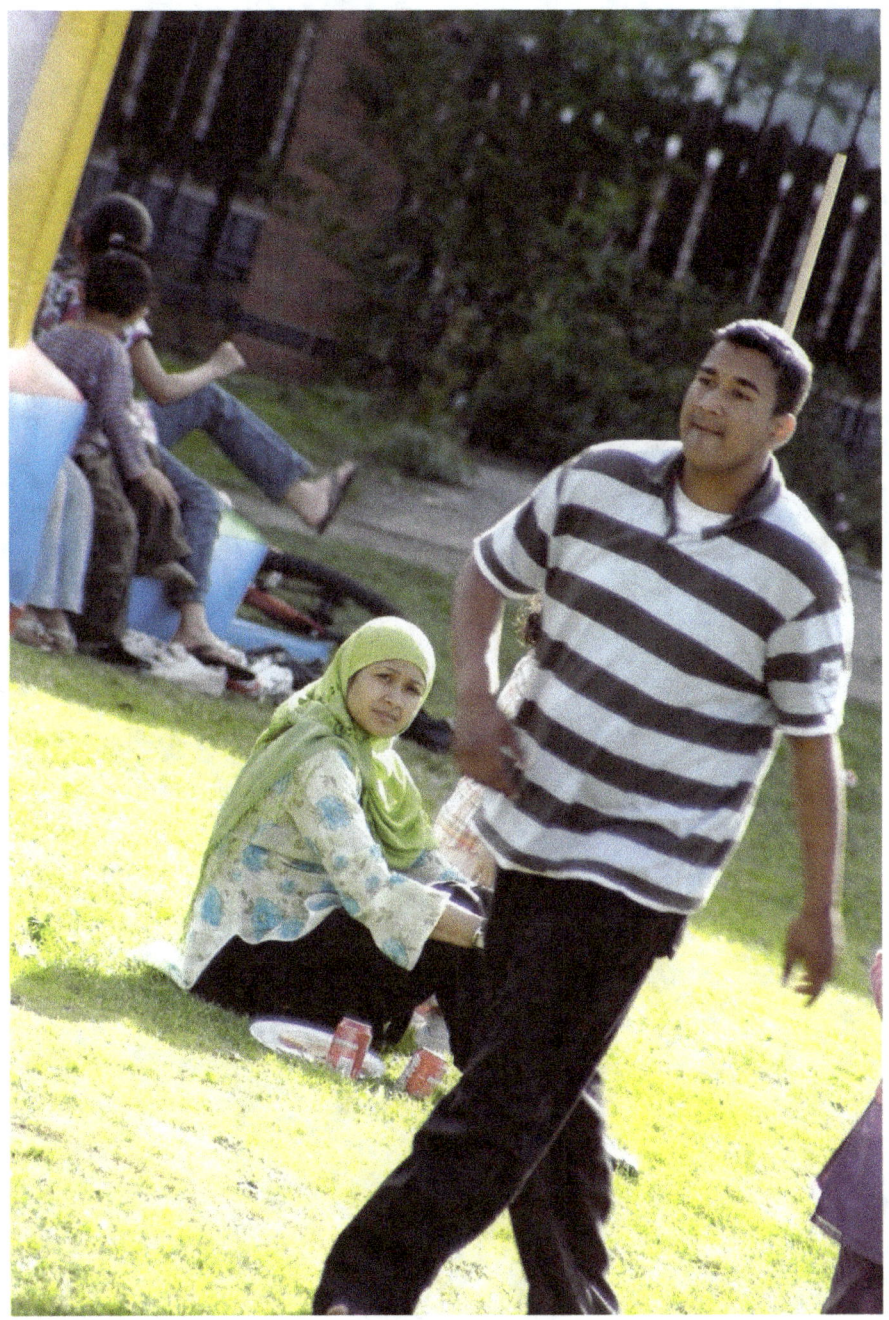

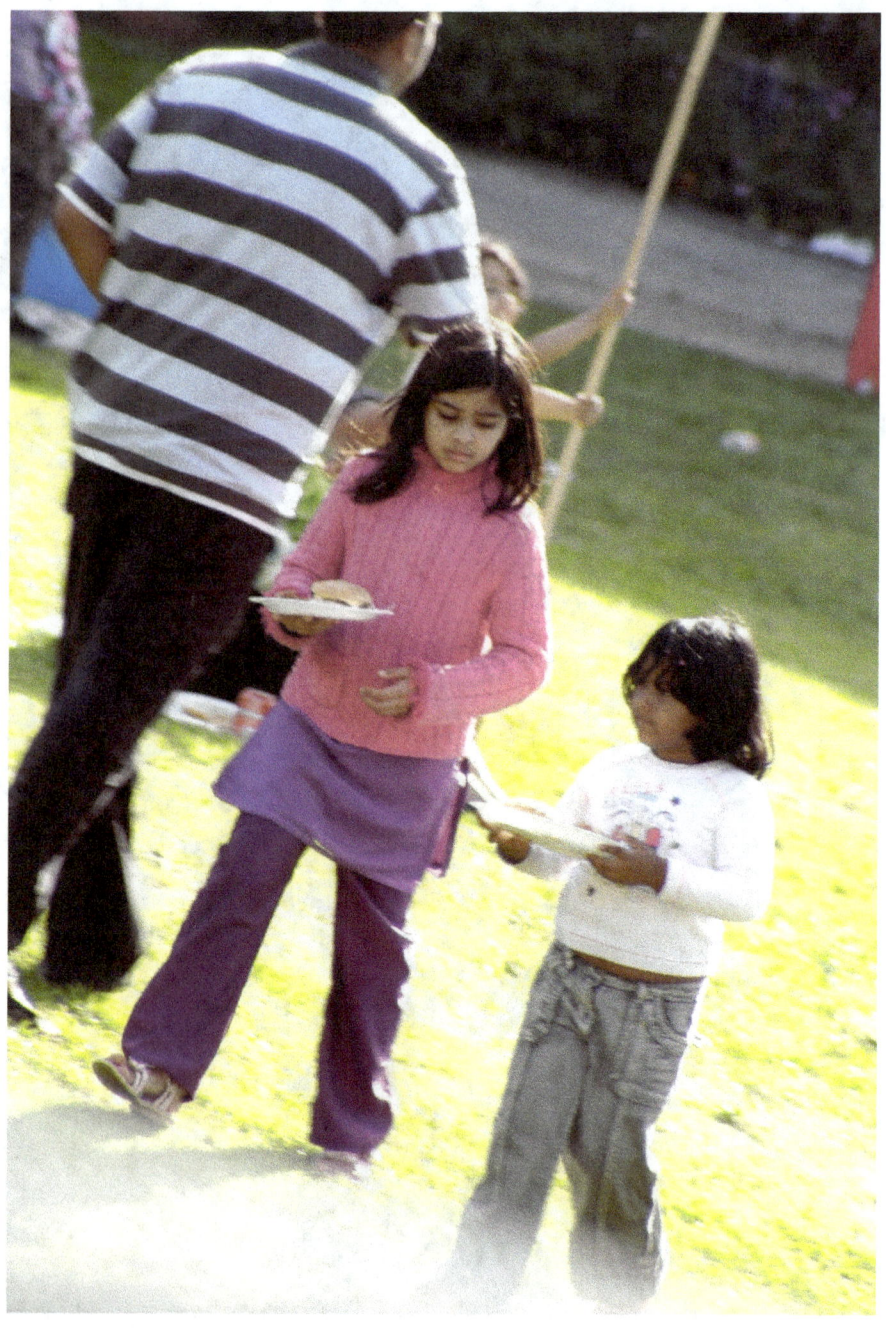

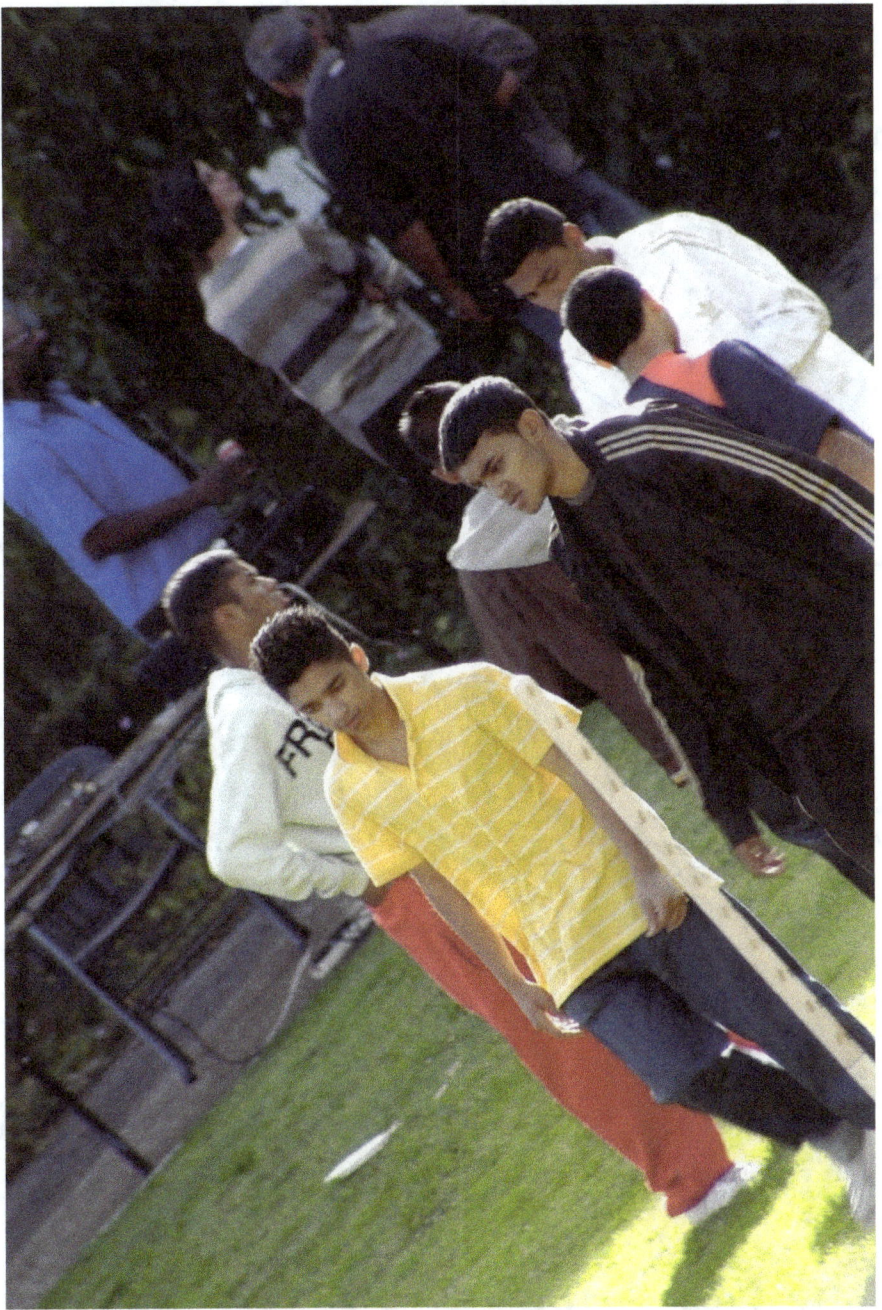

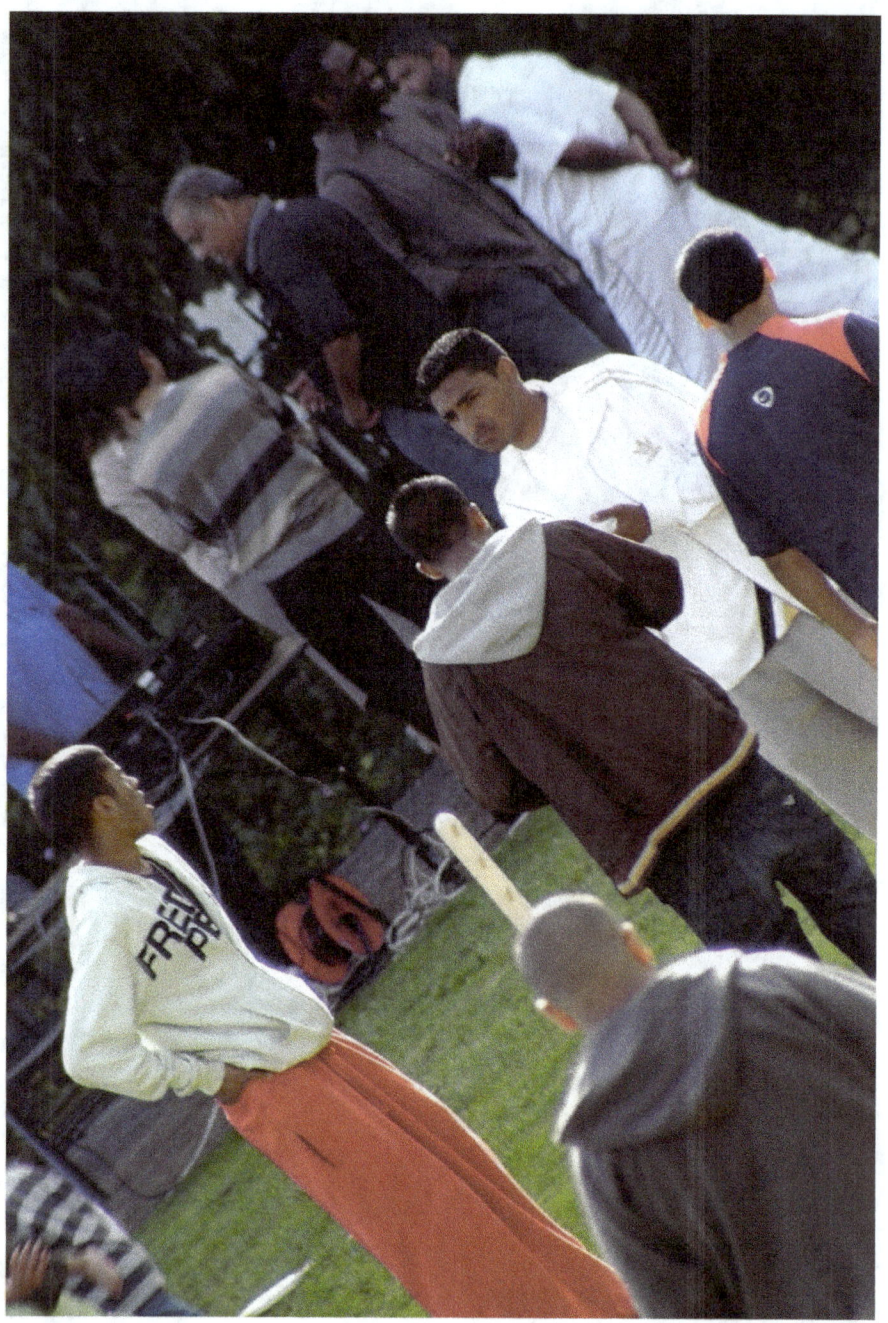

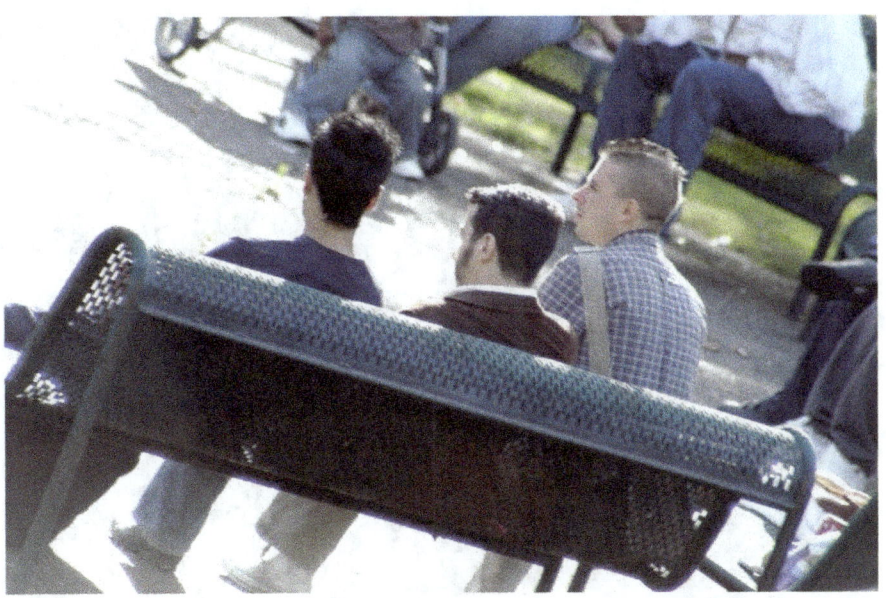

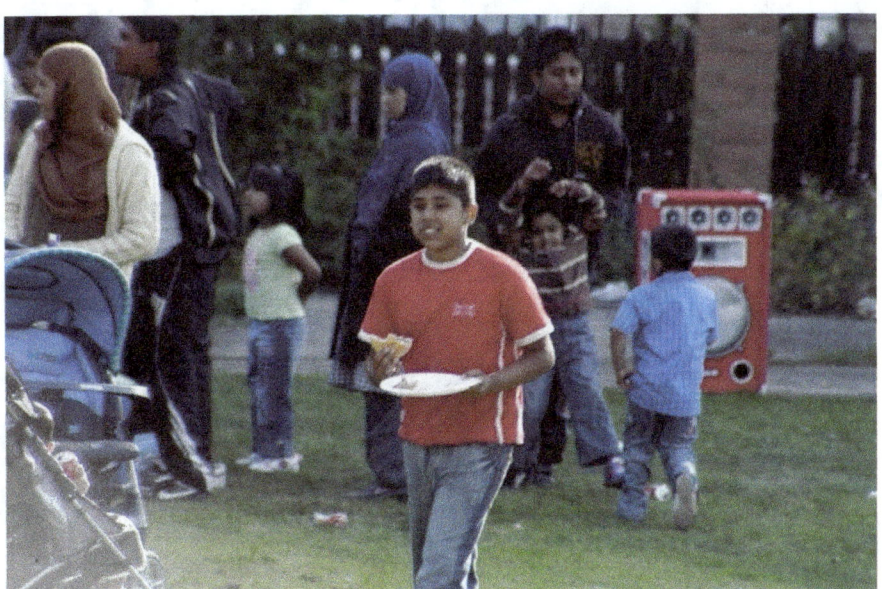

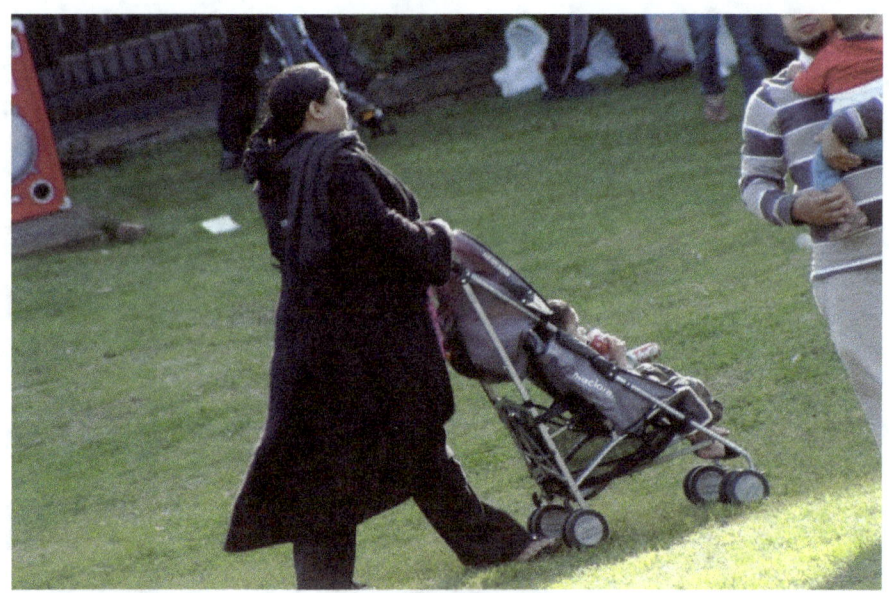

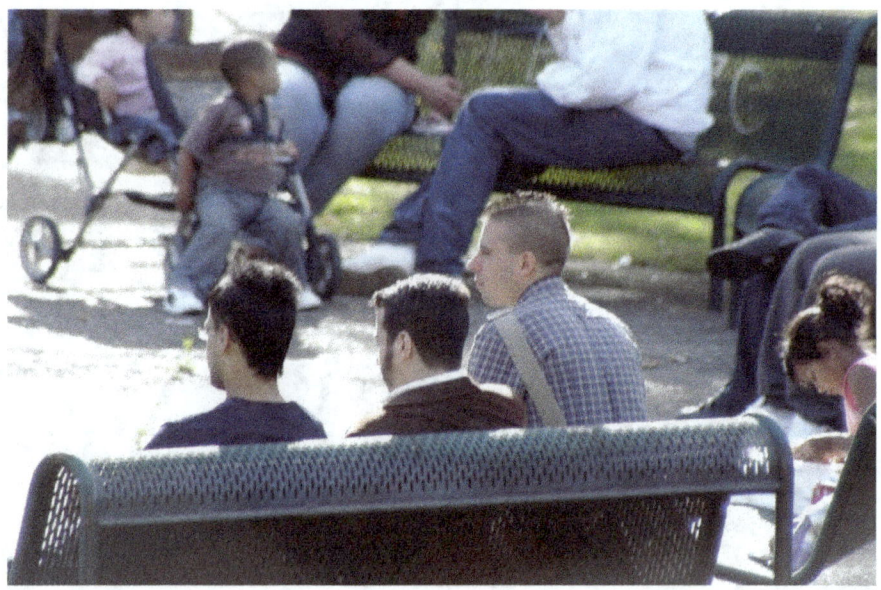

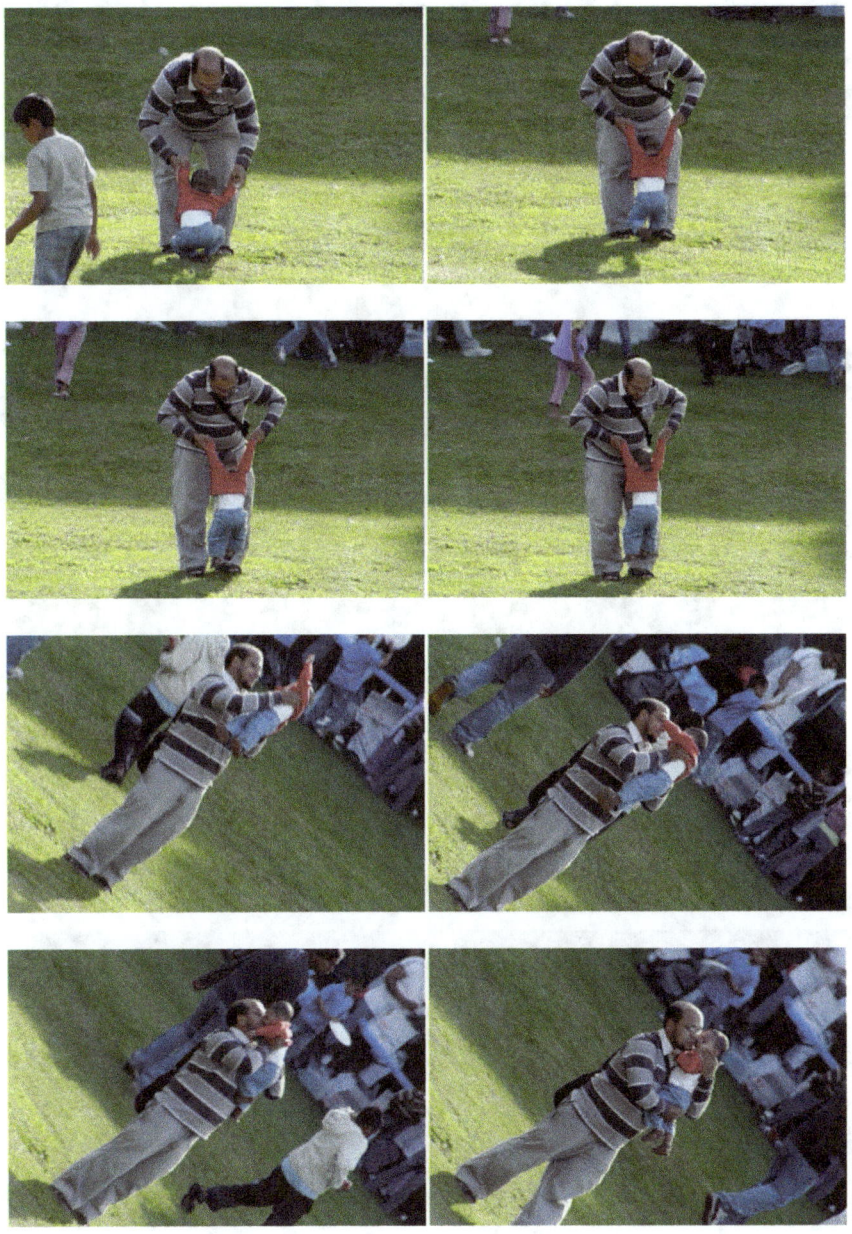

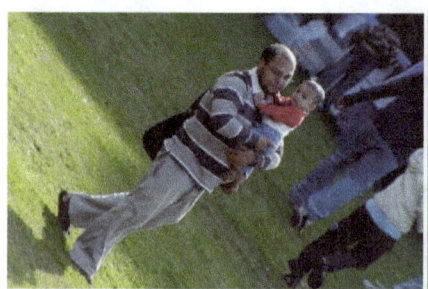
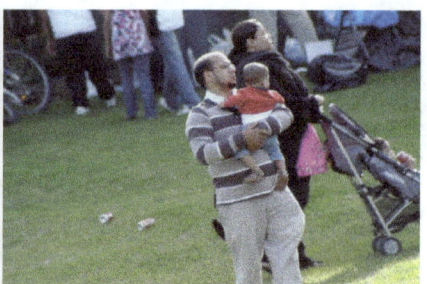

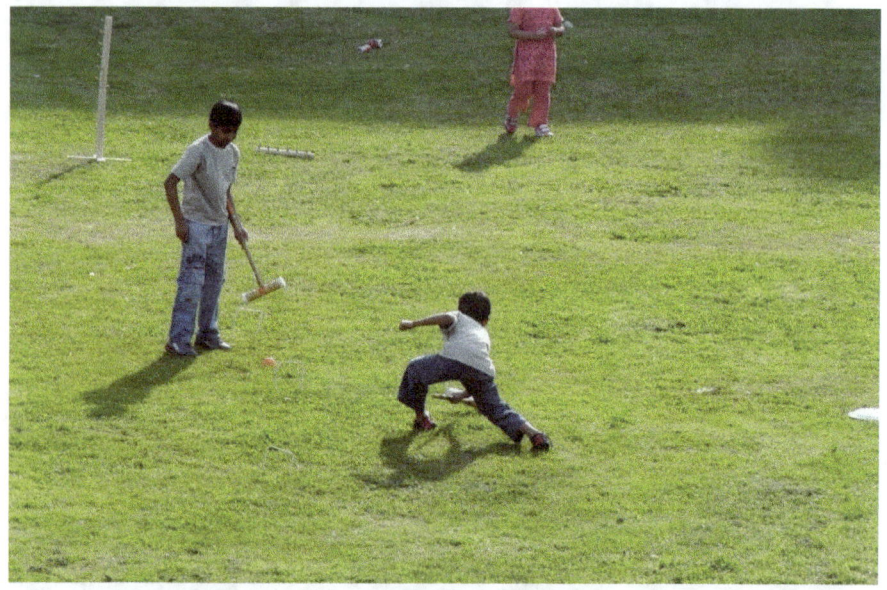

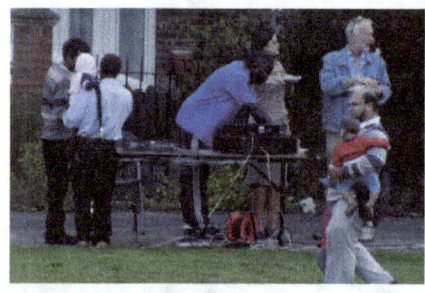
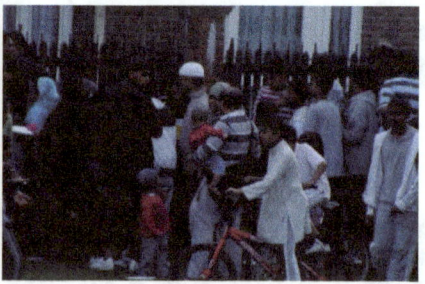

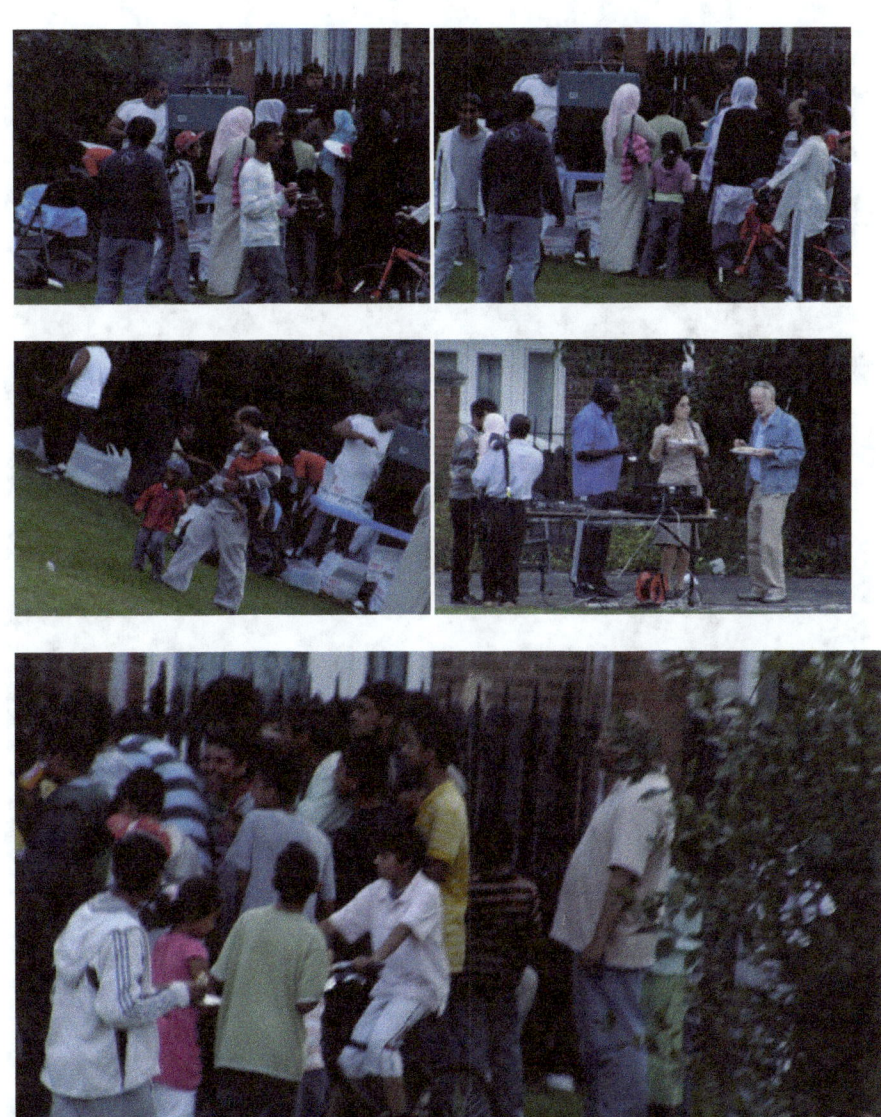

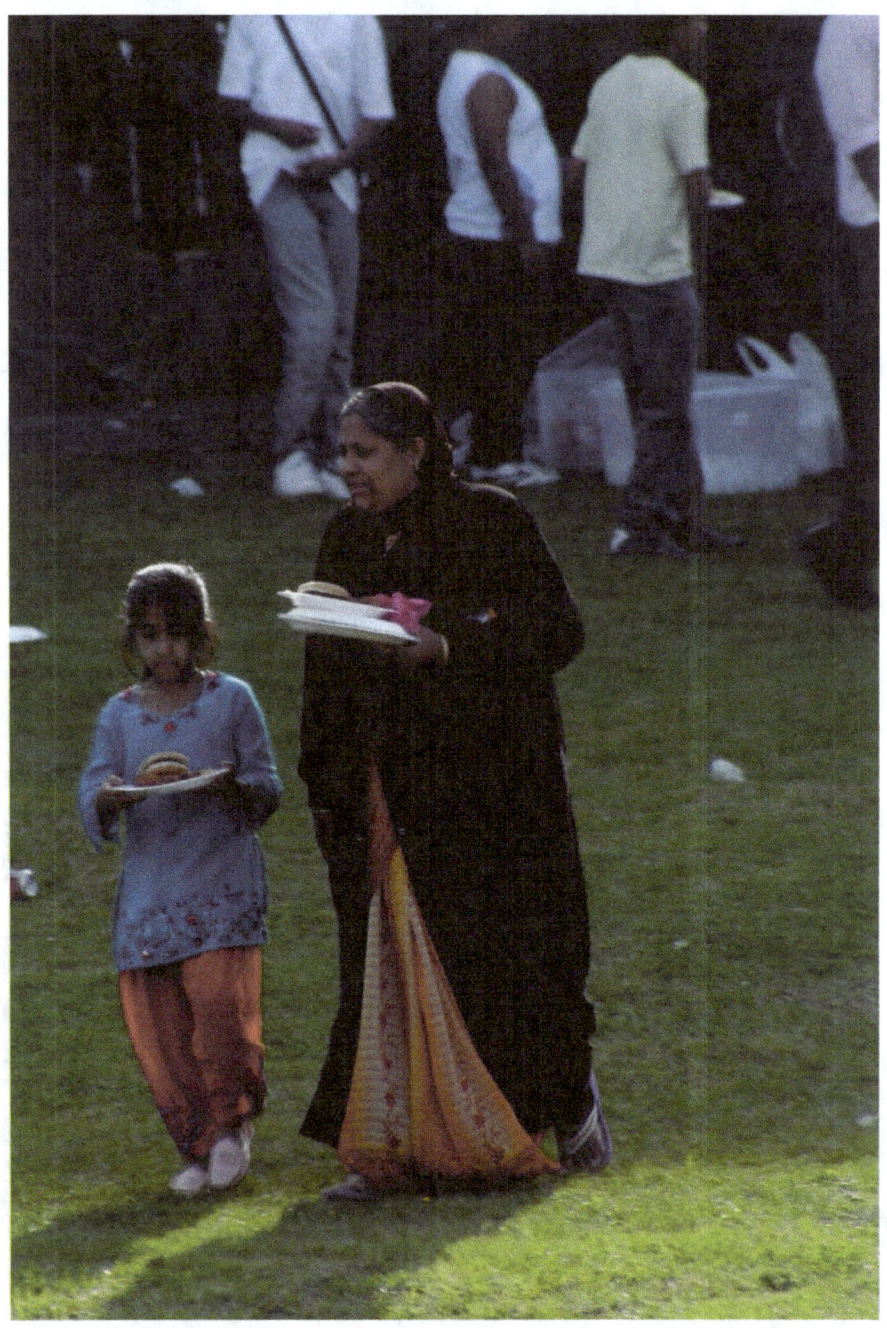

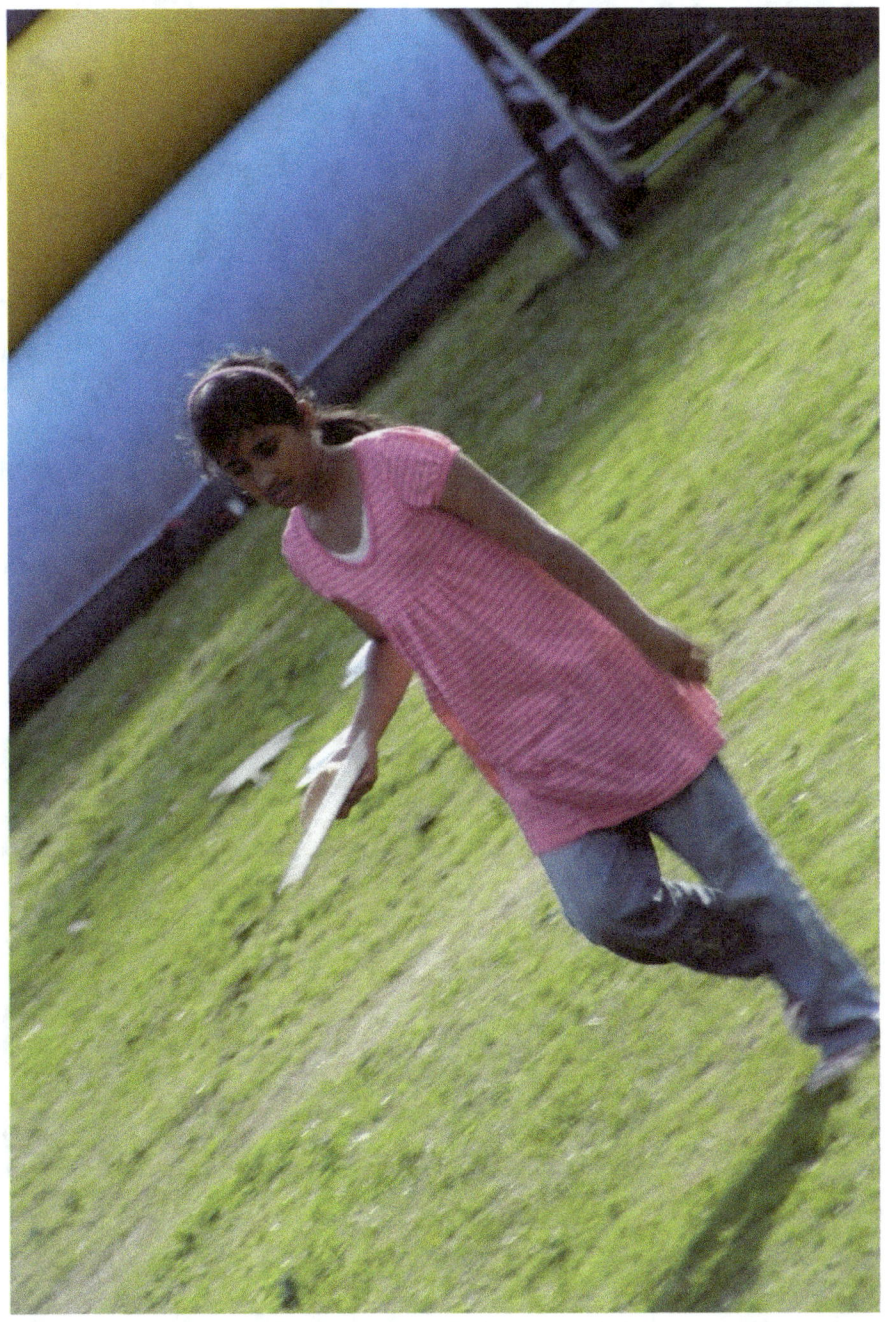

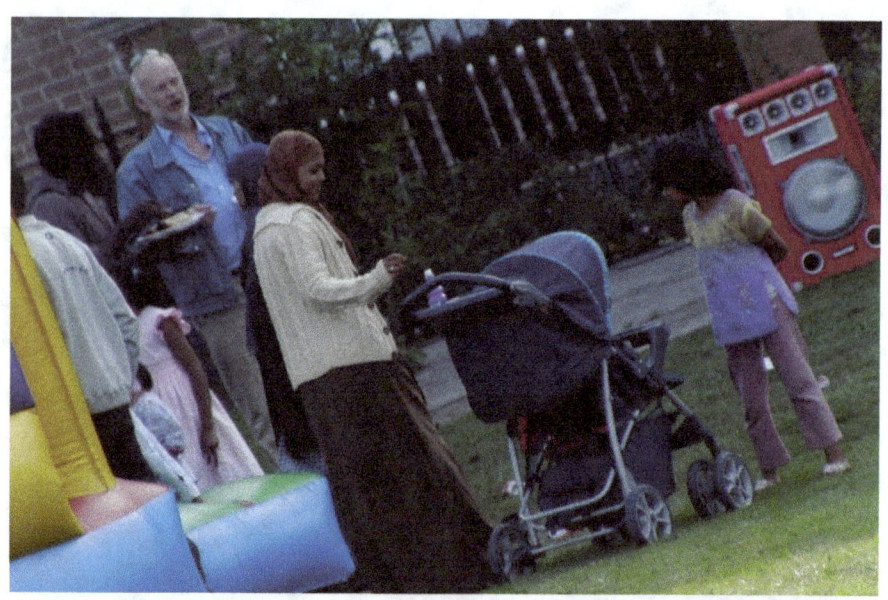

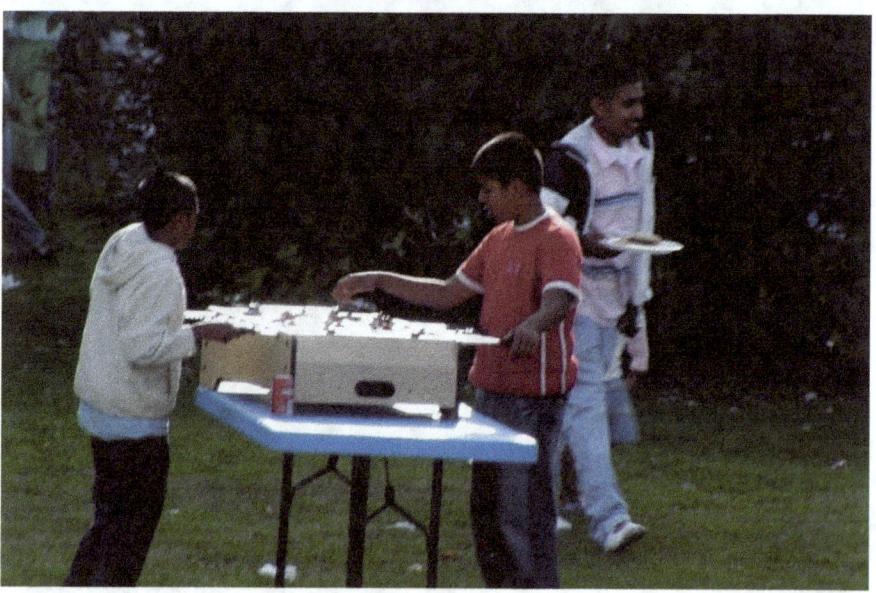

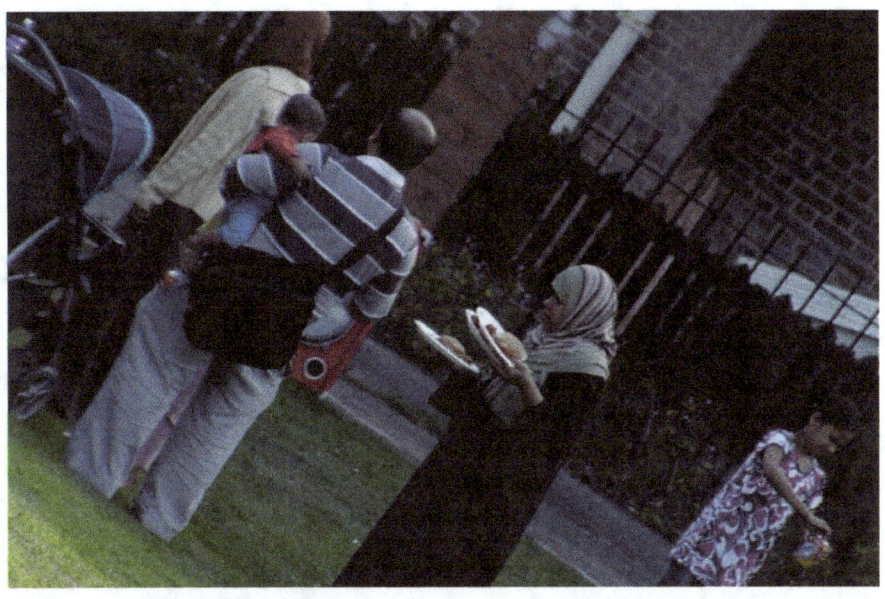

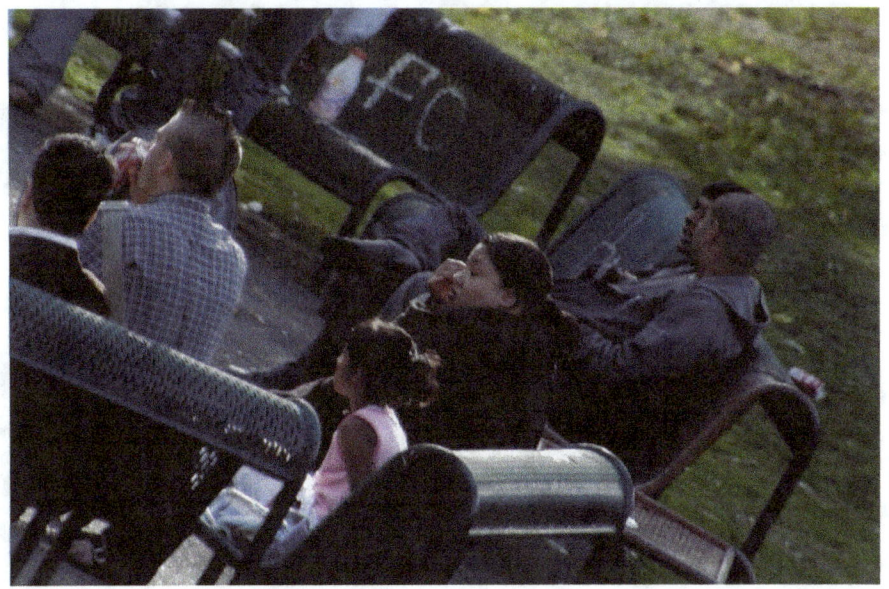

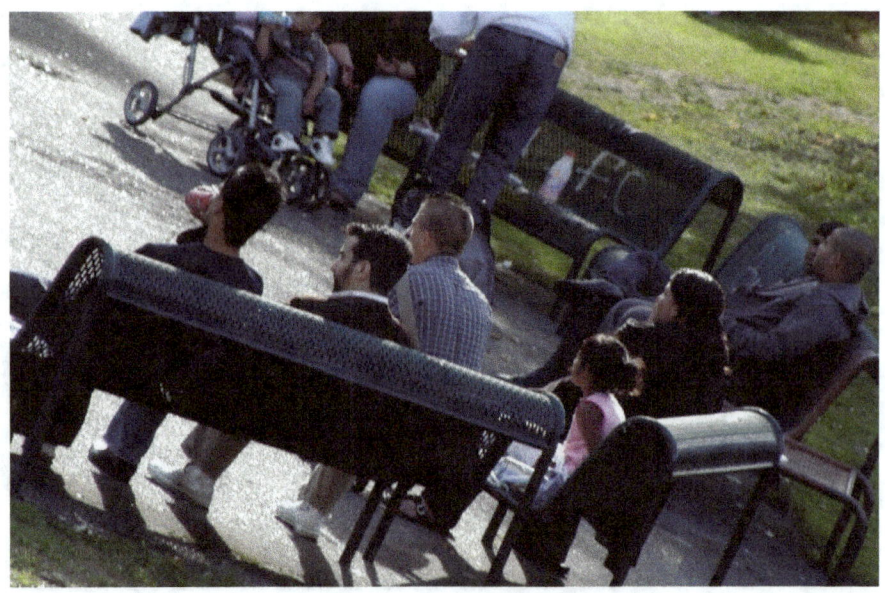

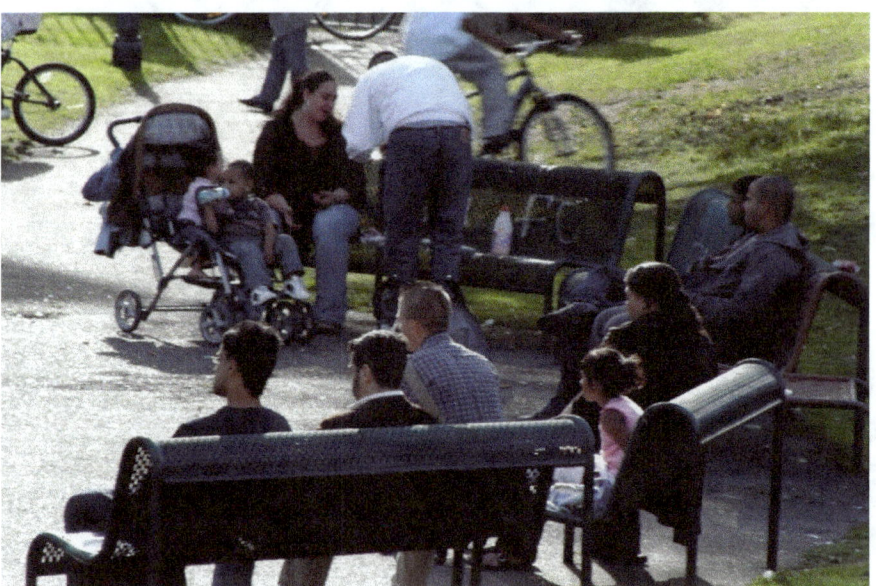

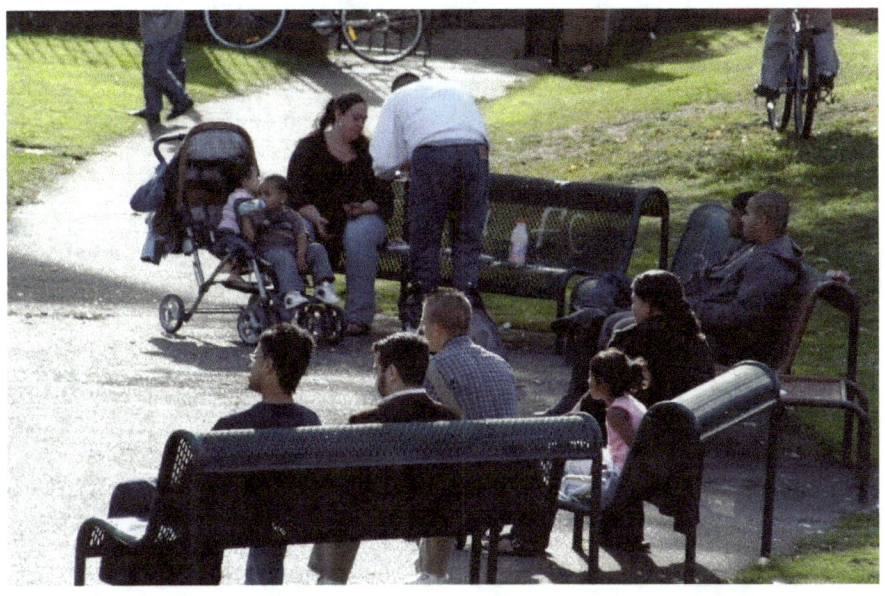

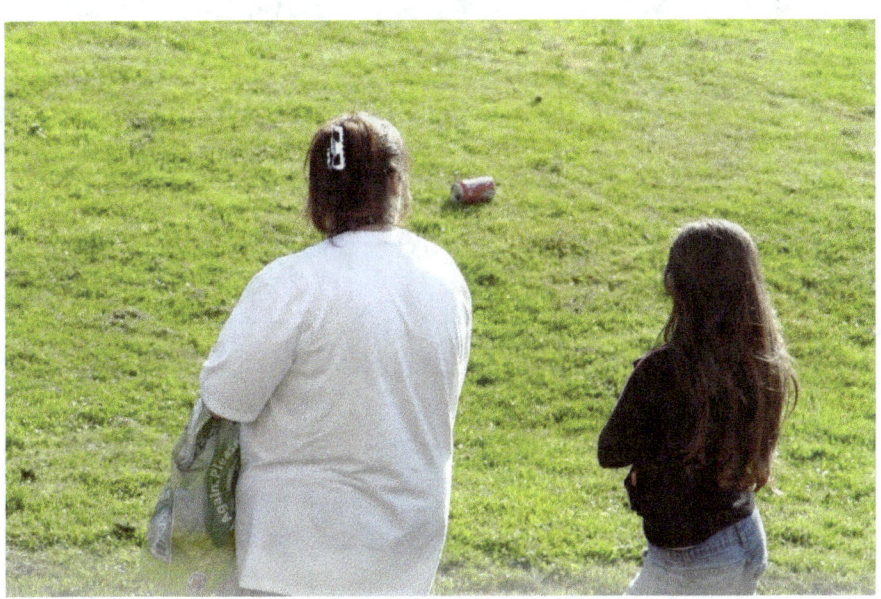

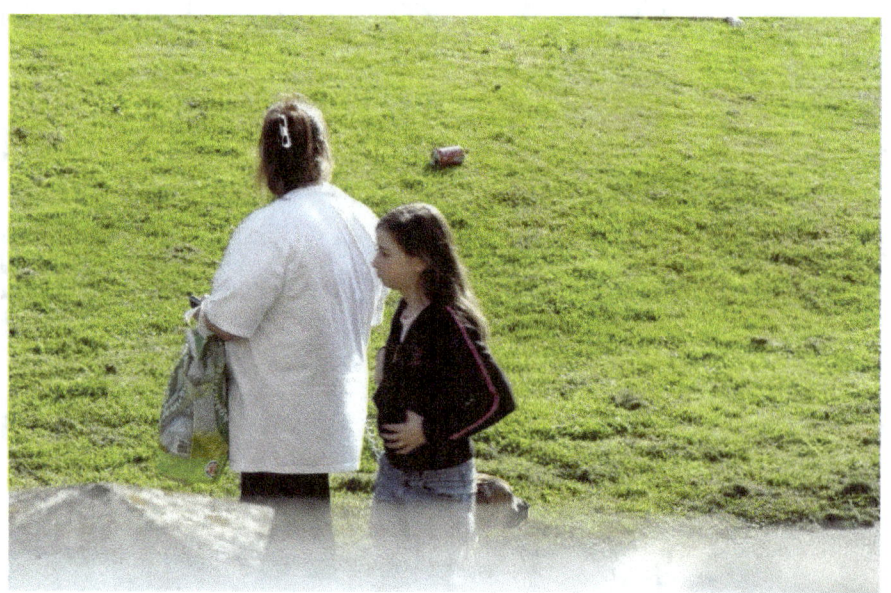

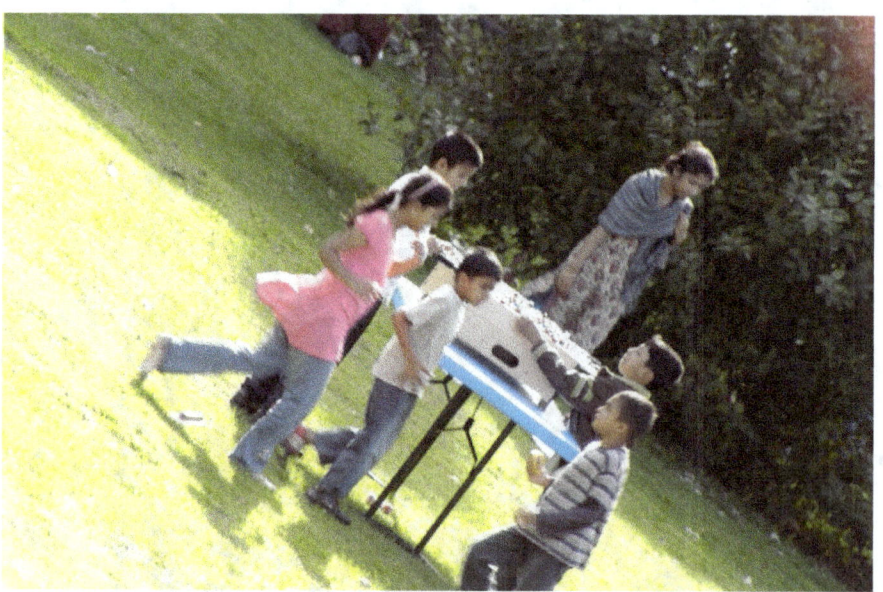

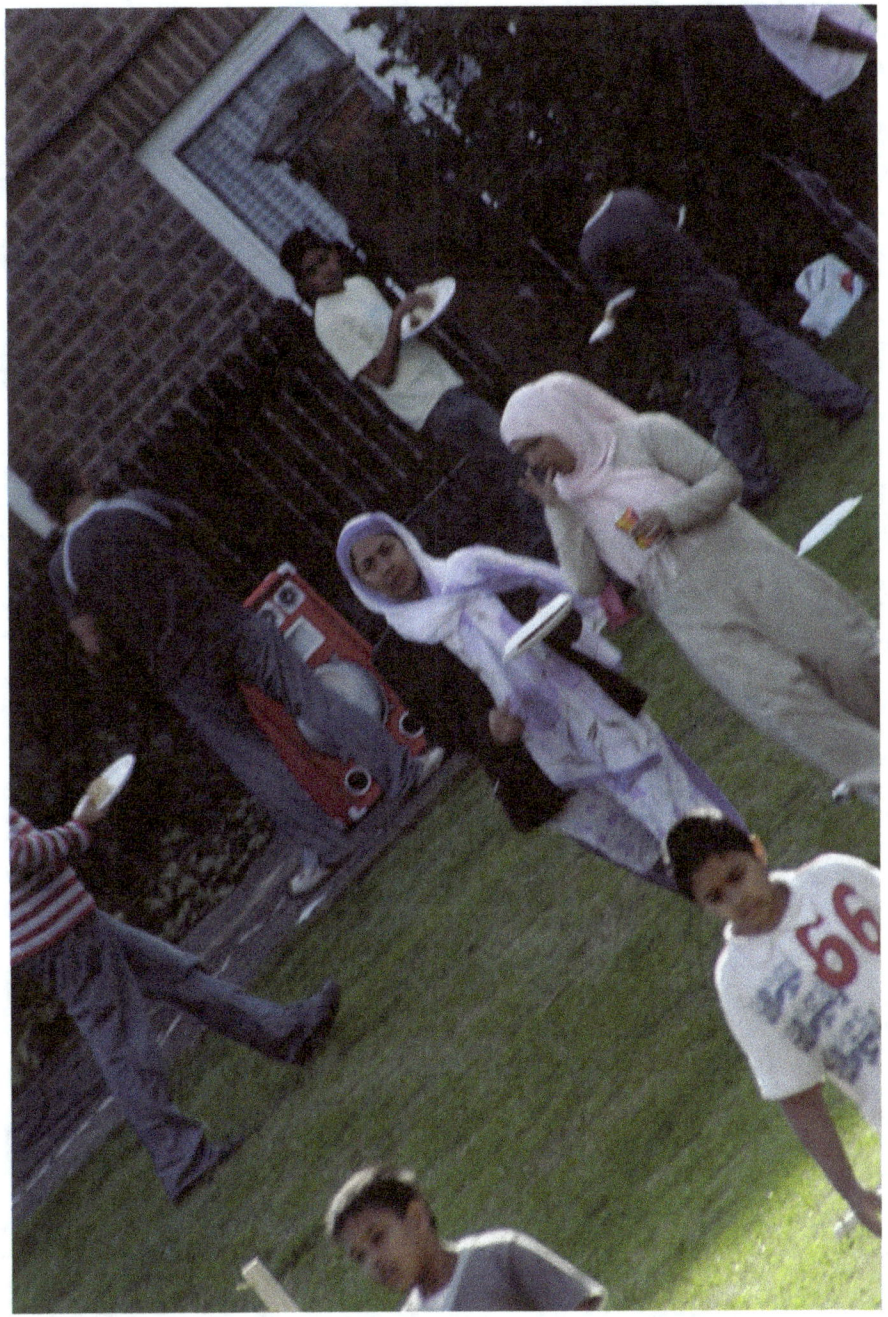

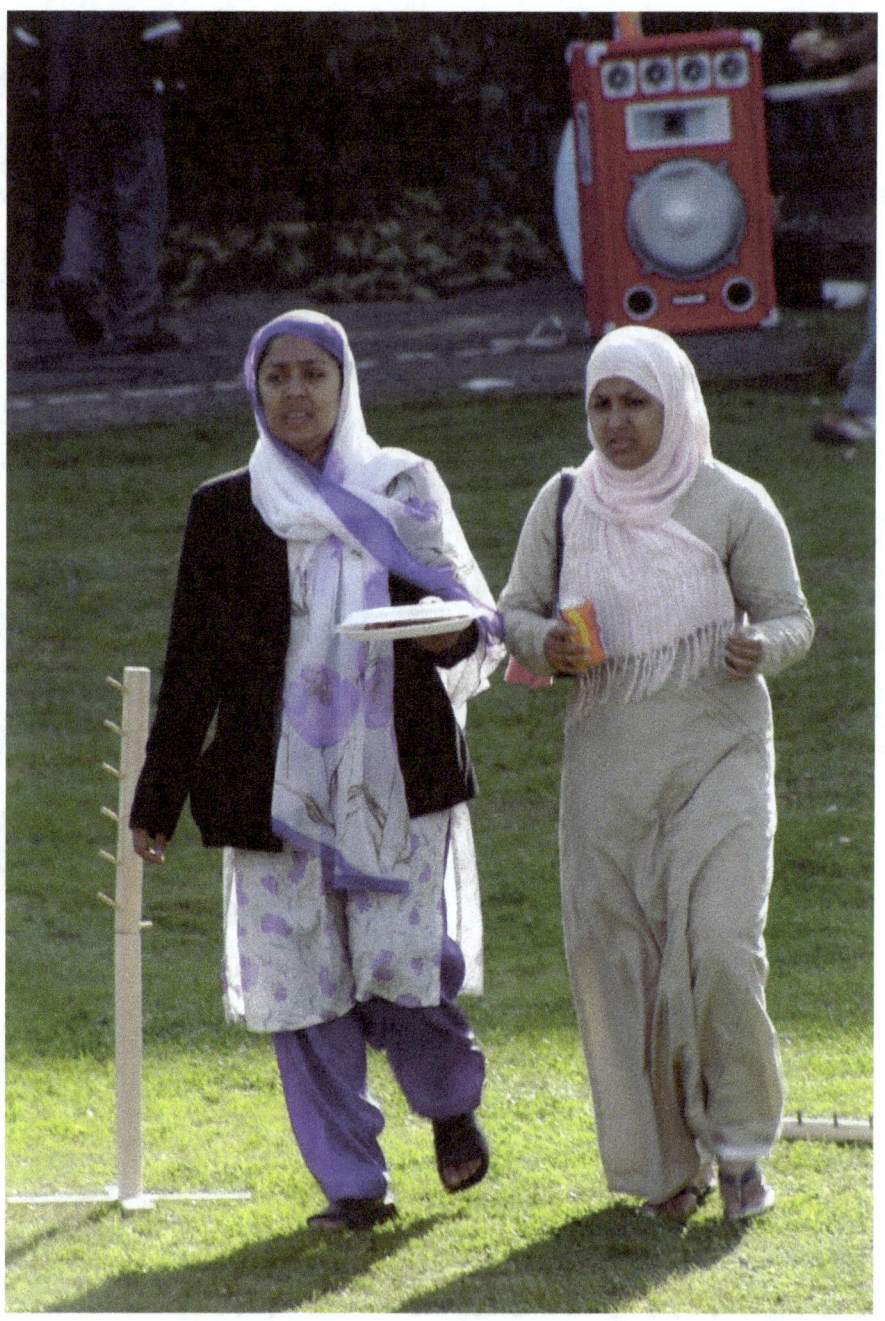

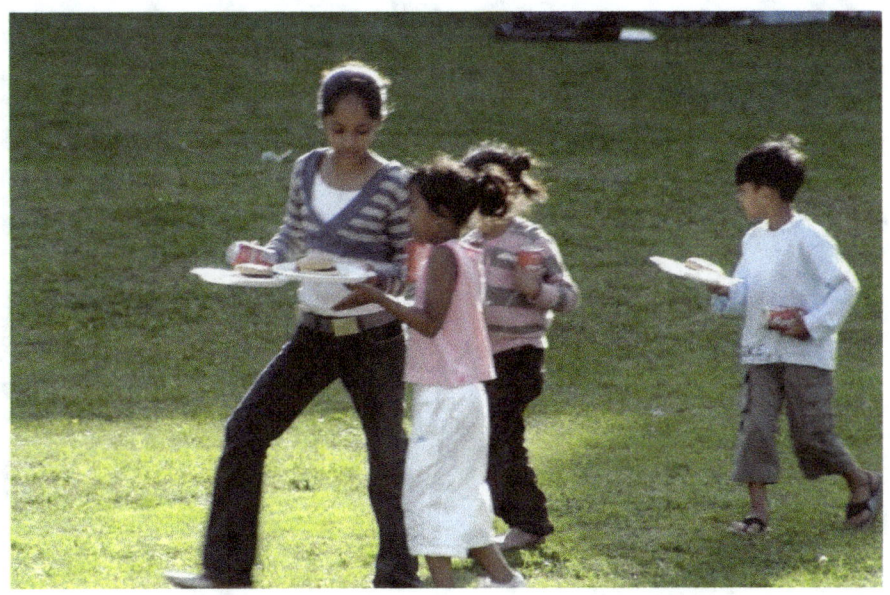

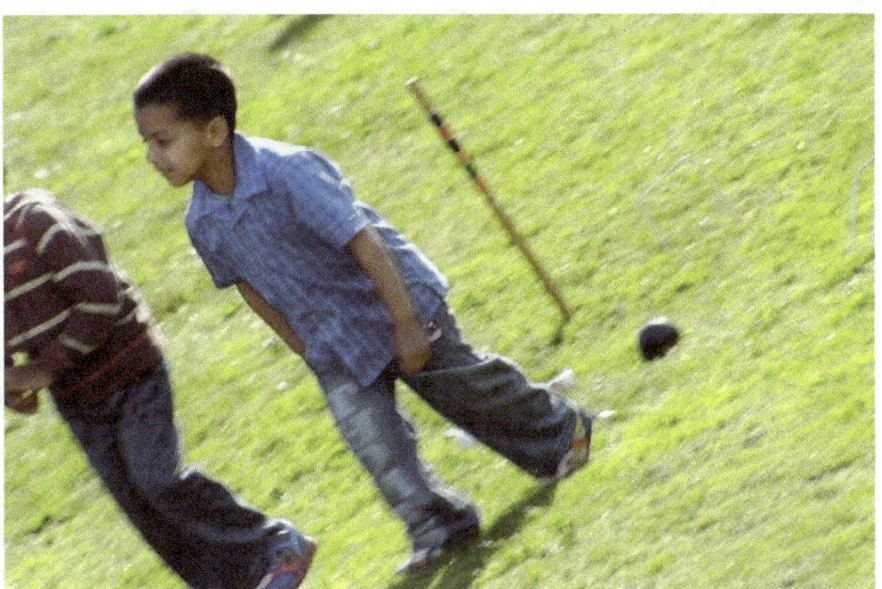

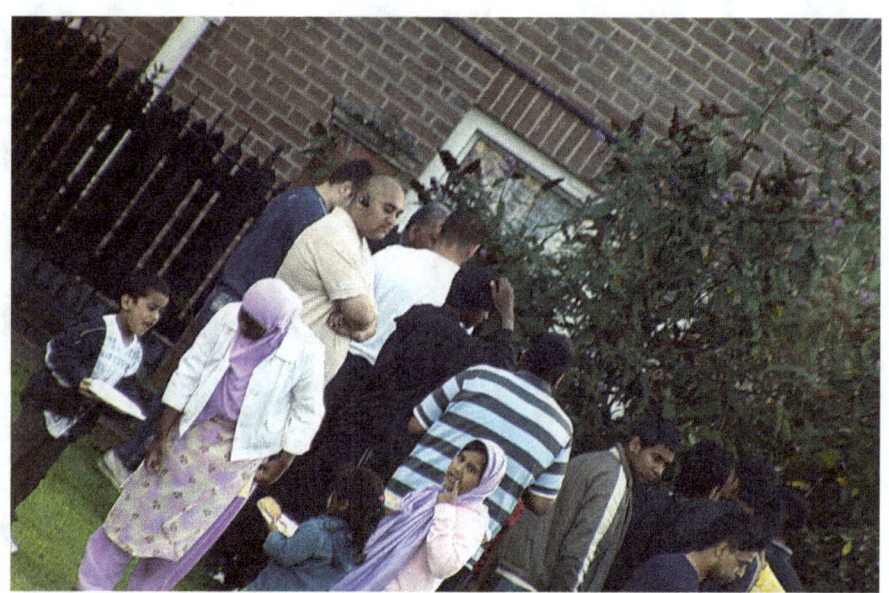

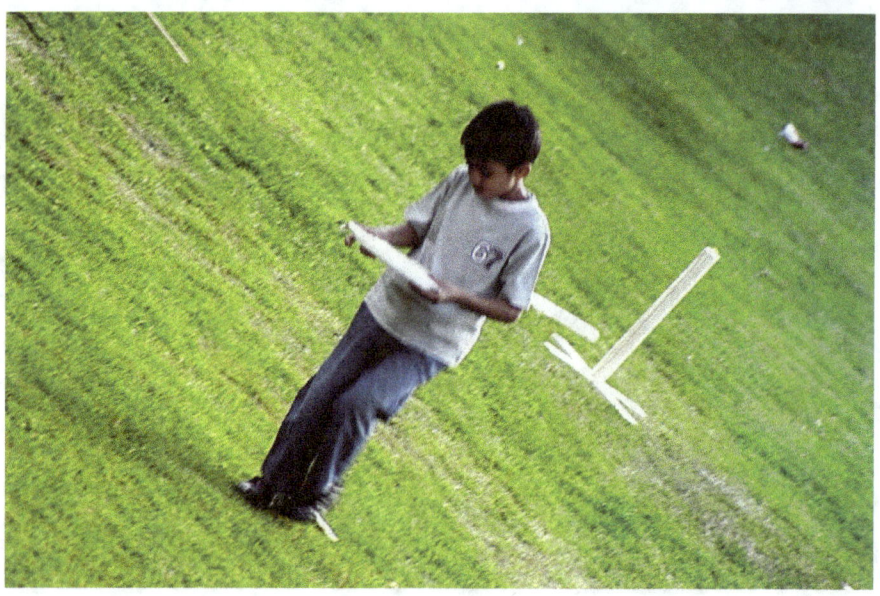

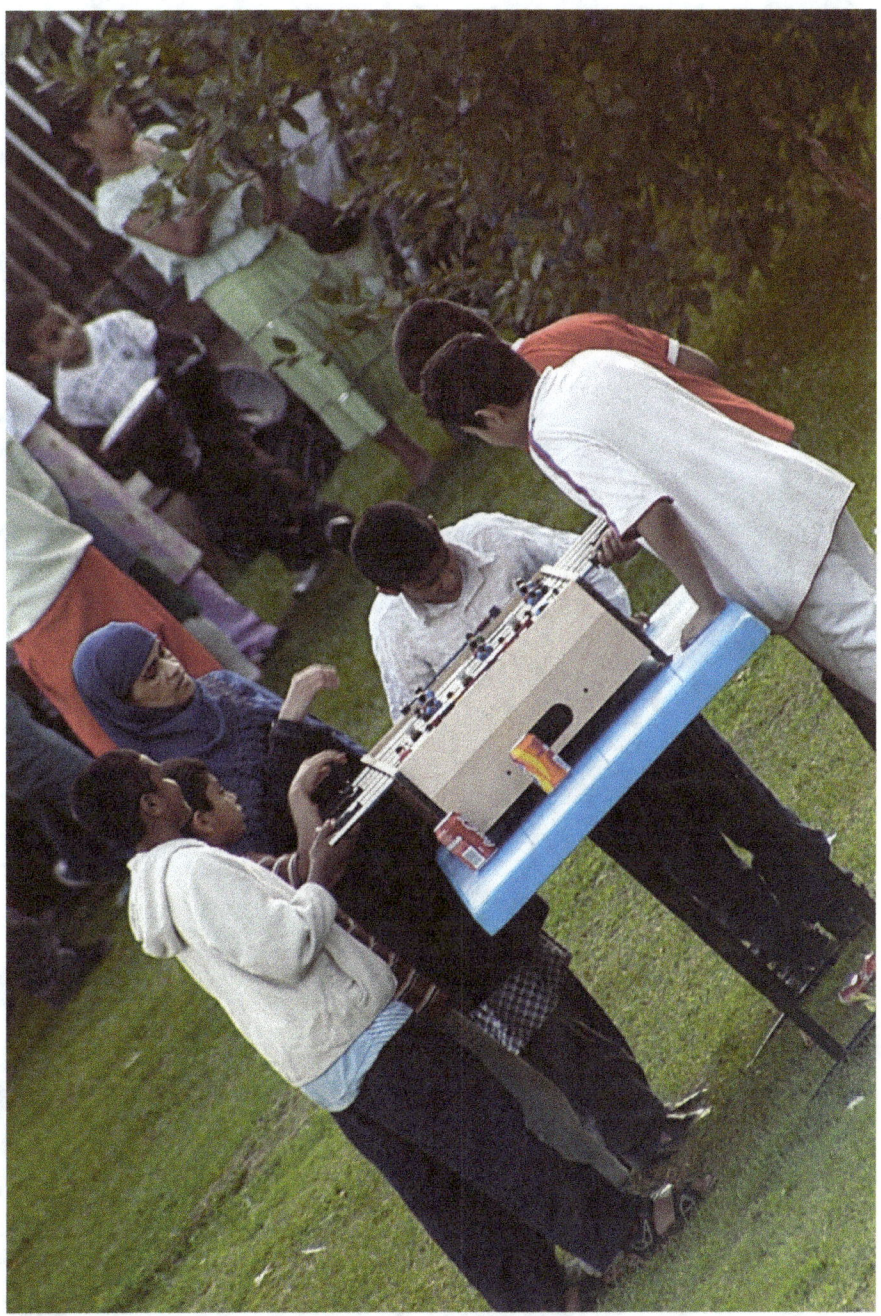

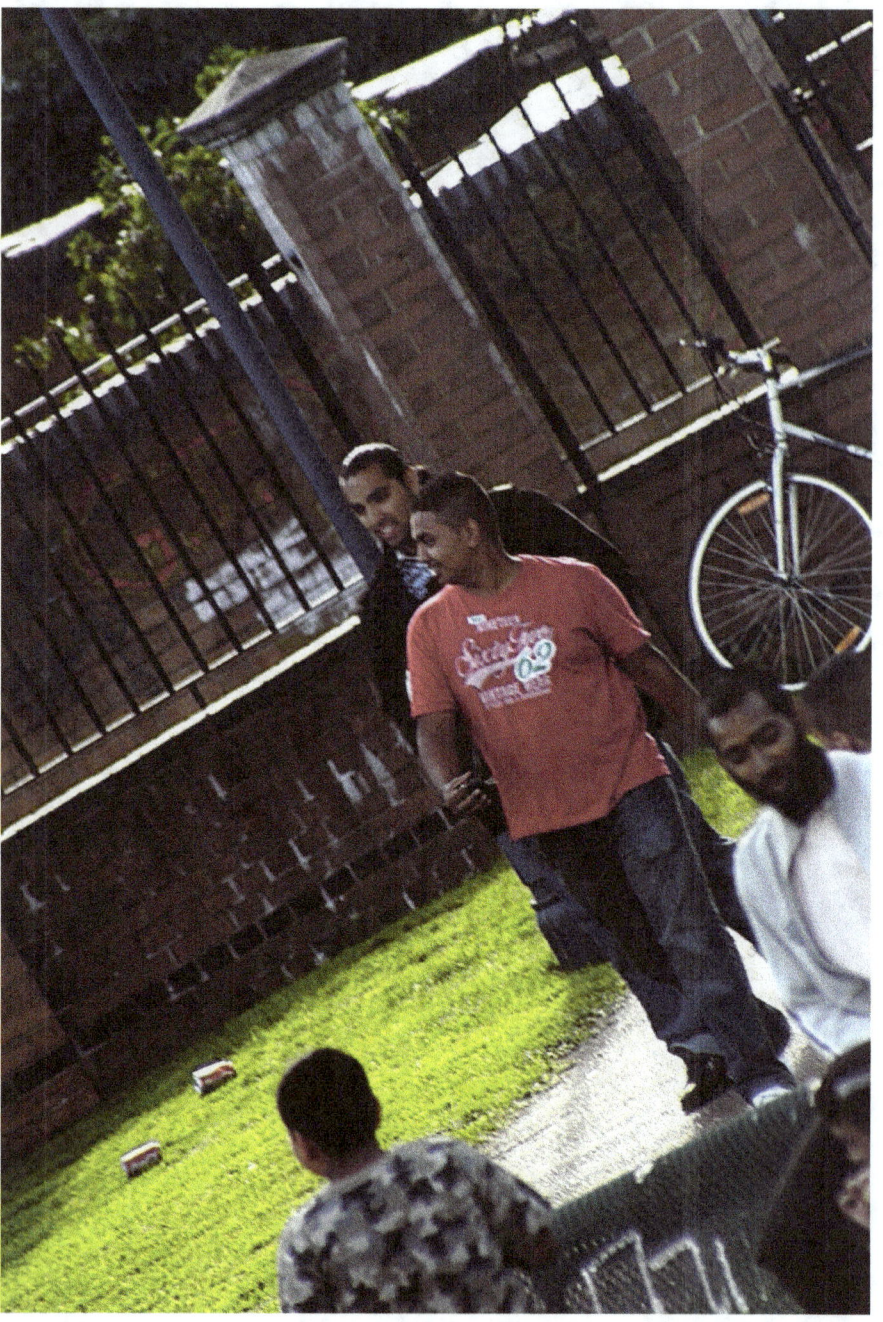

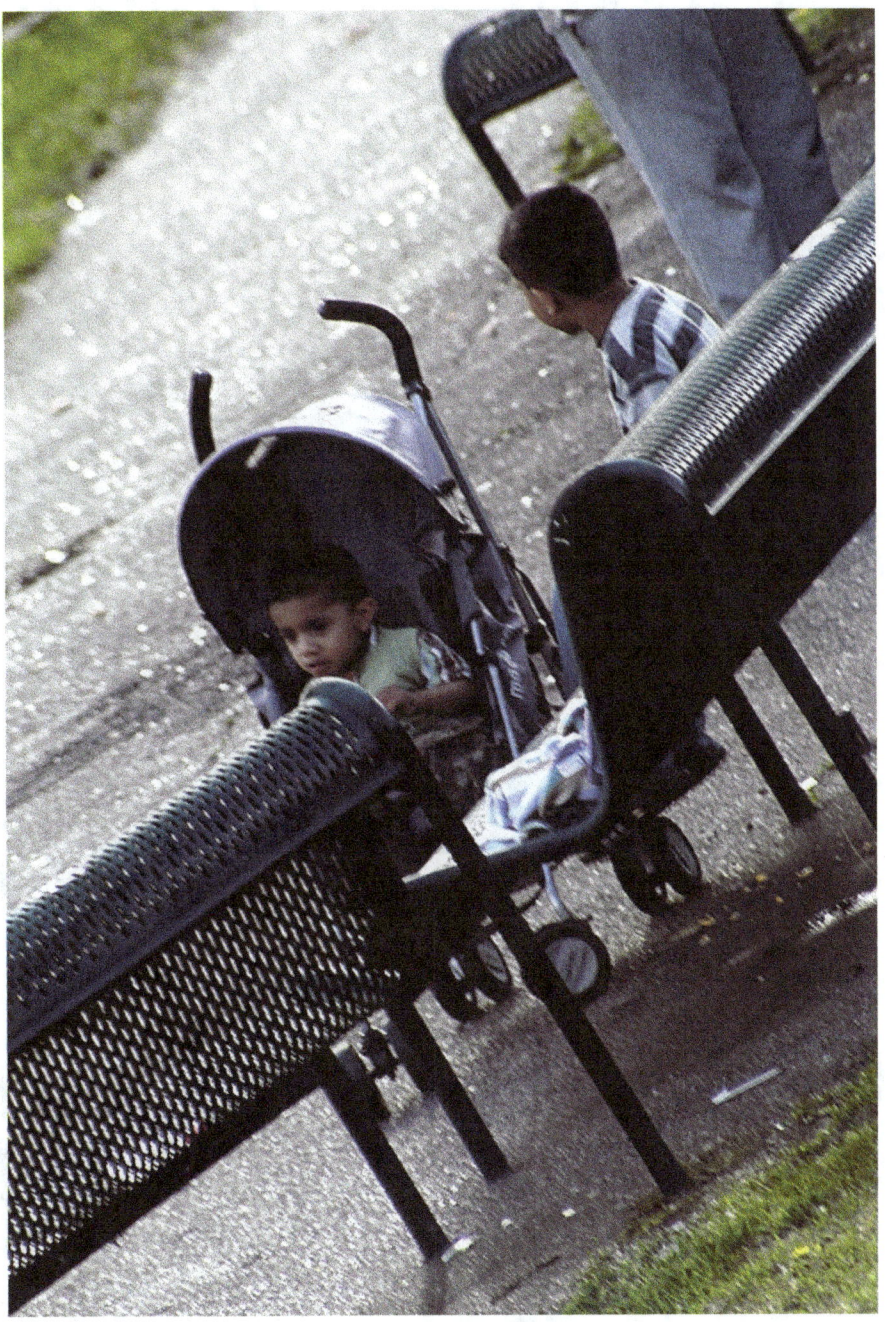

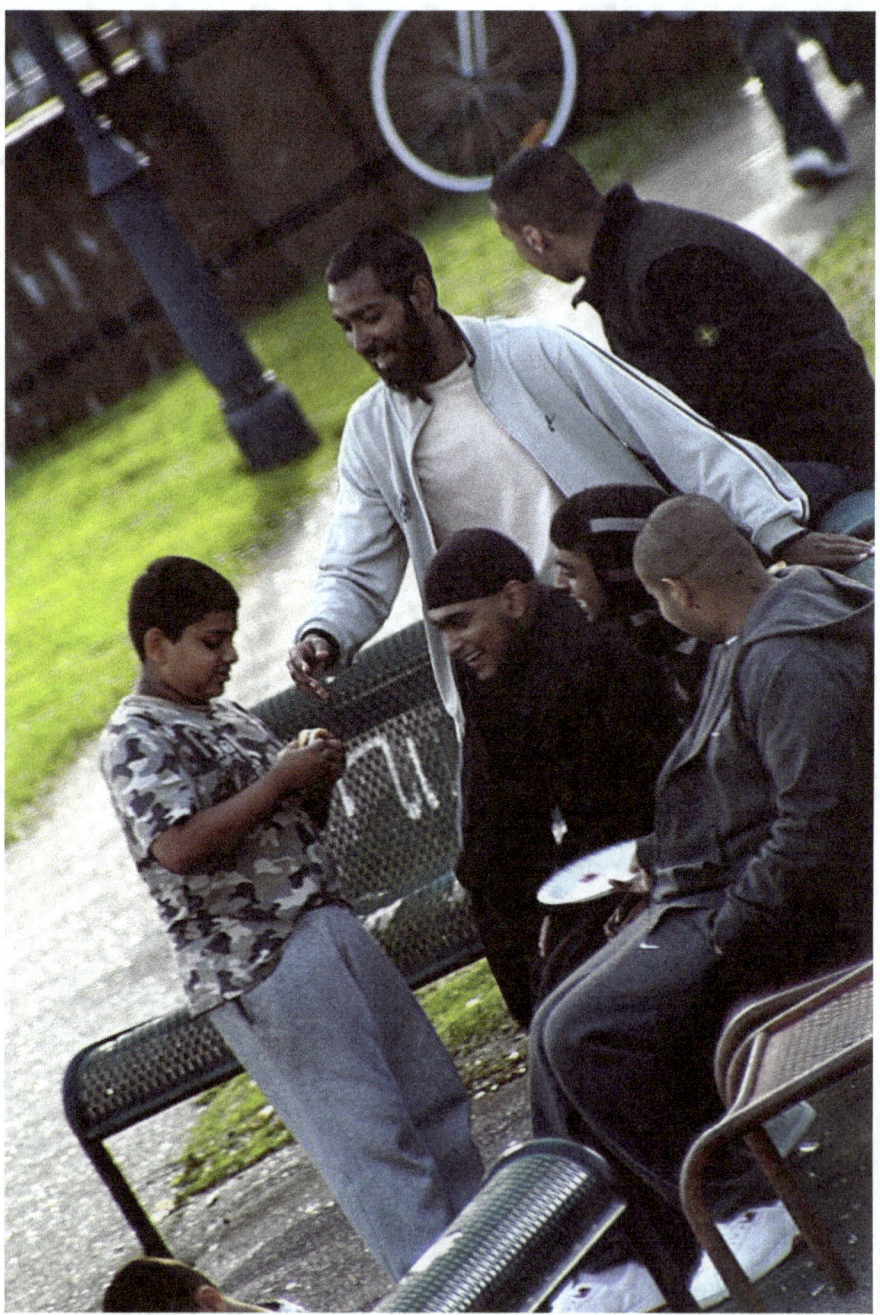

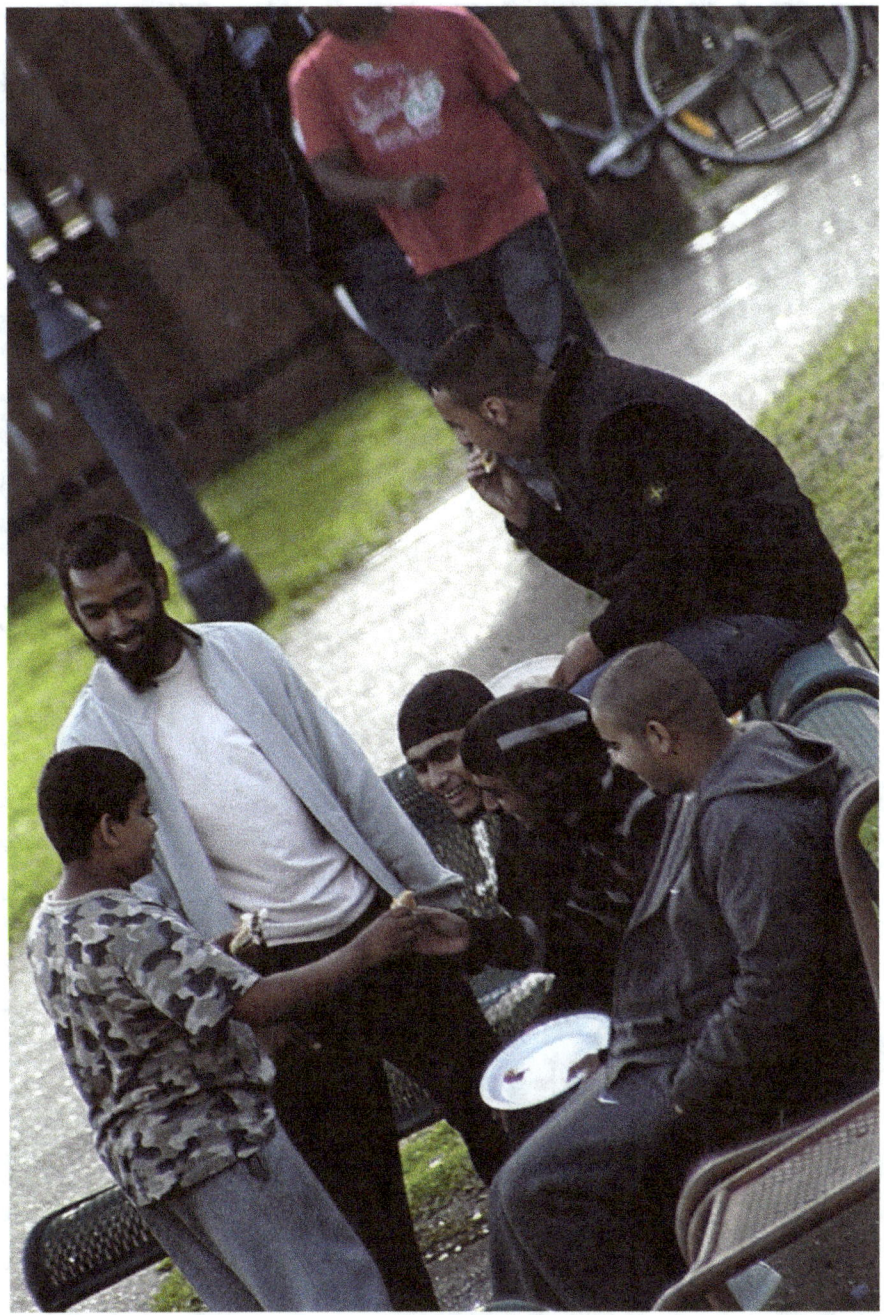

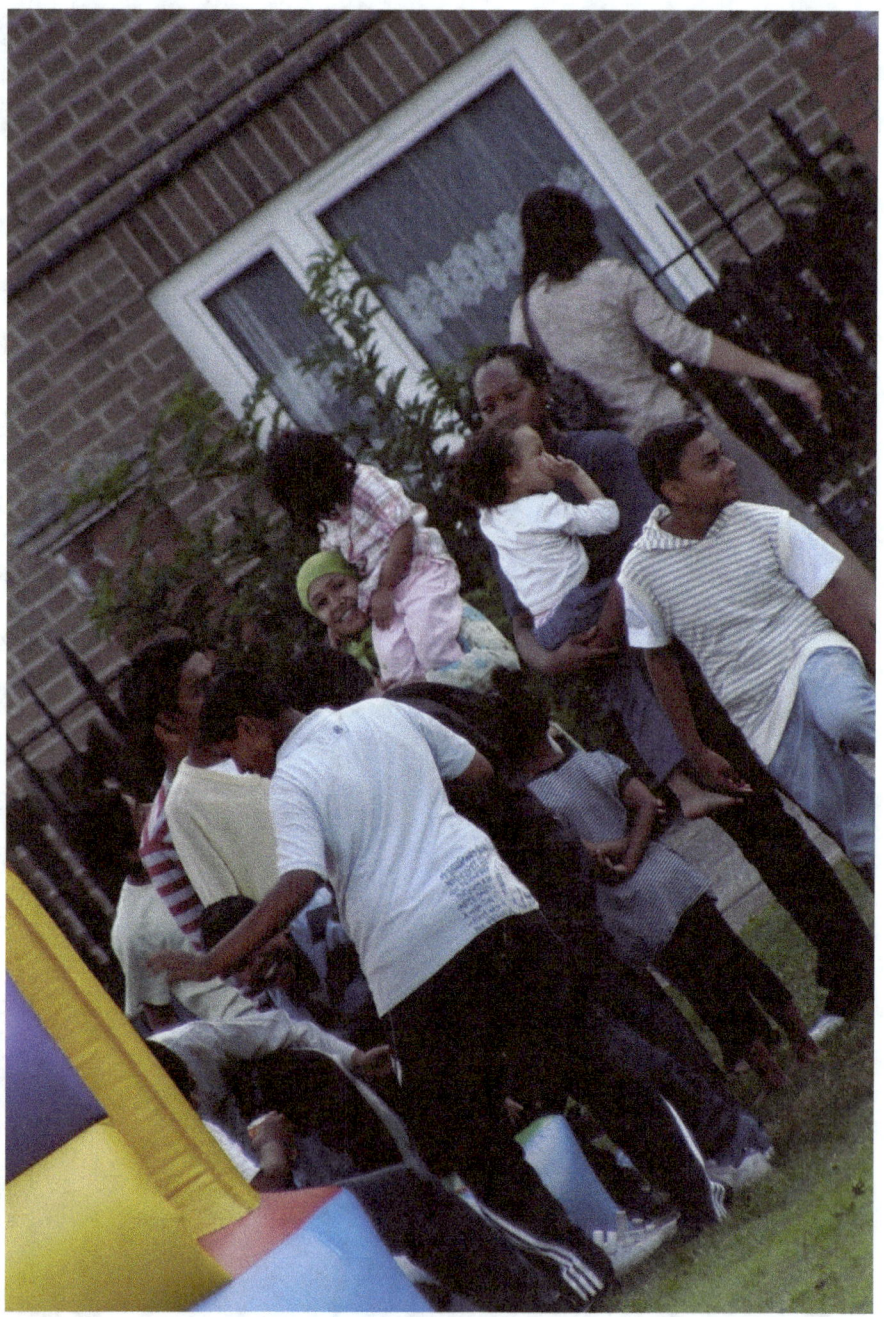

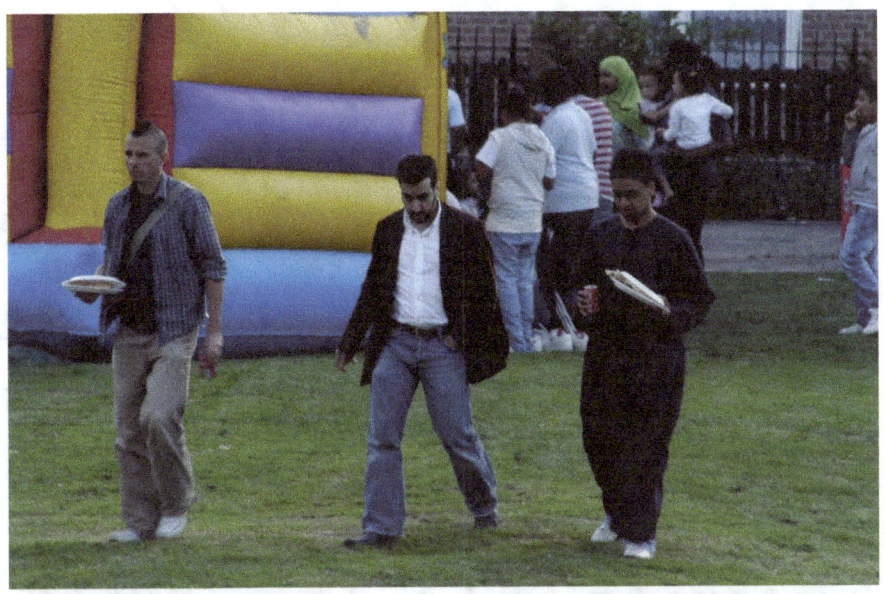

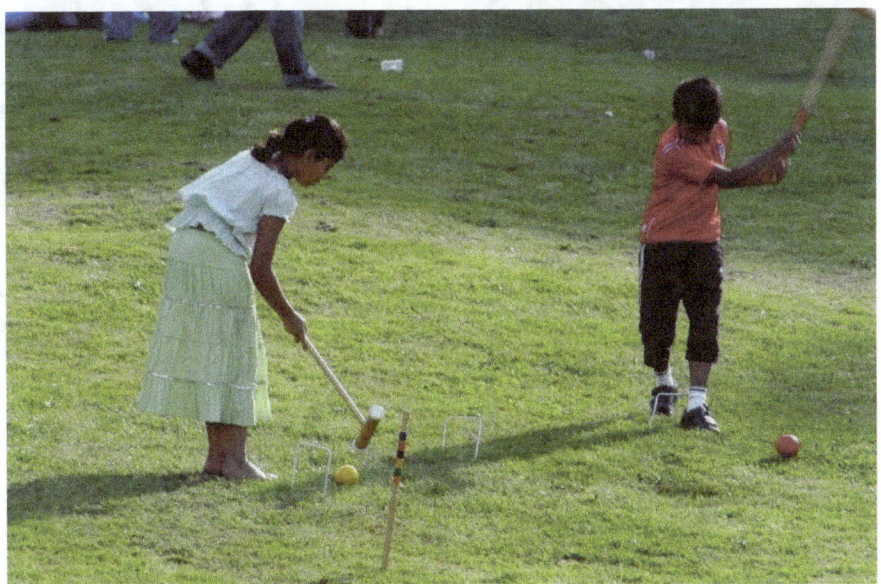

Boys & Girls having a go..

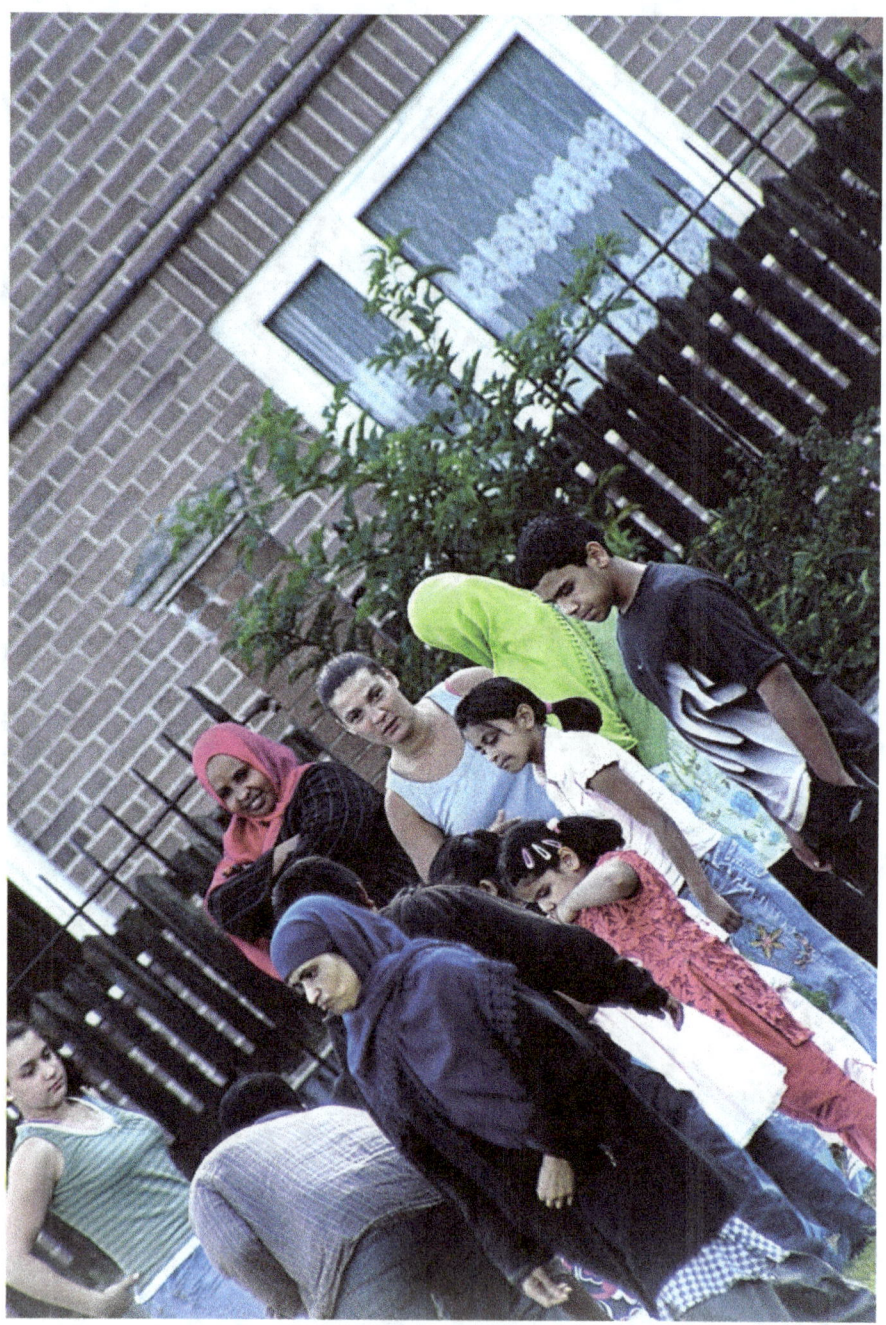

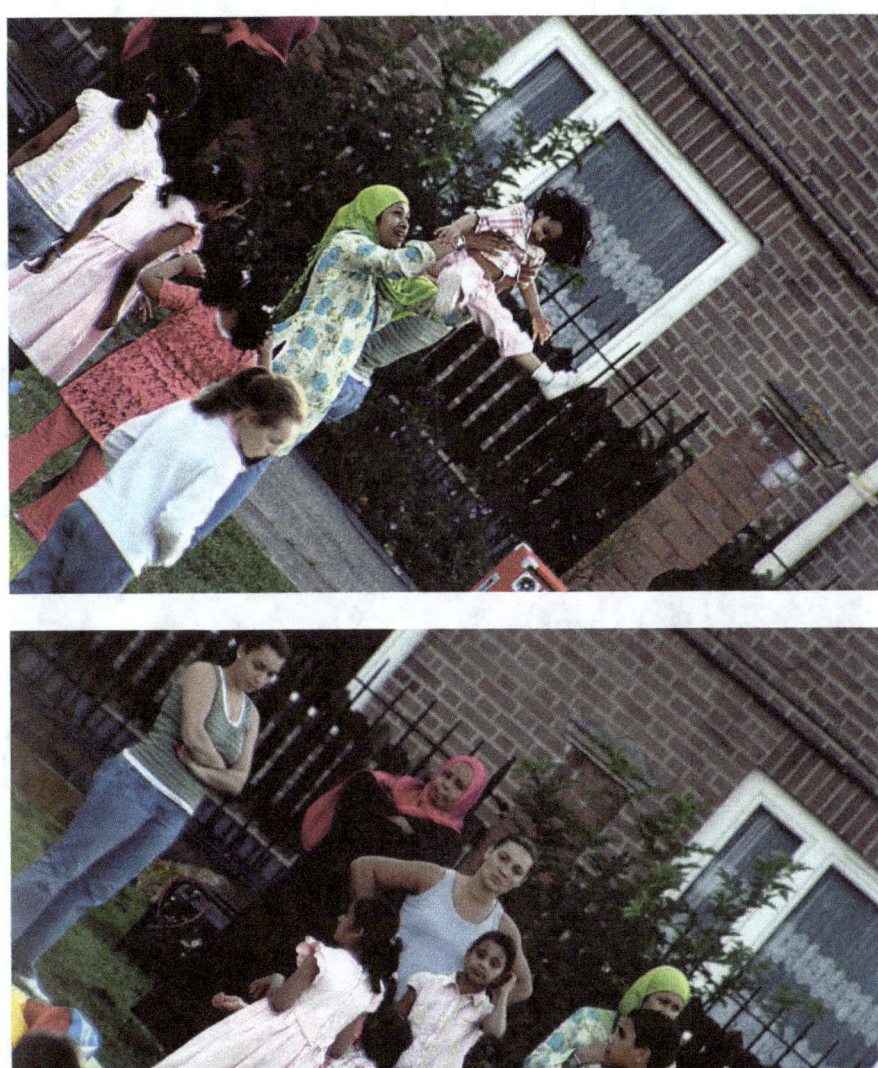

Non Bangladeshi and Somalian family out mingling sharing the days event.

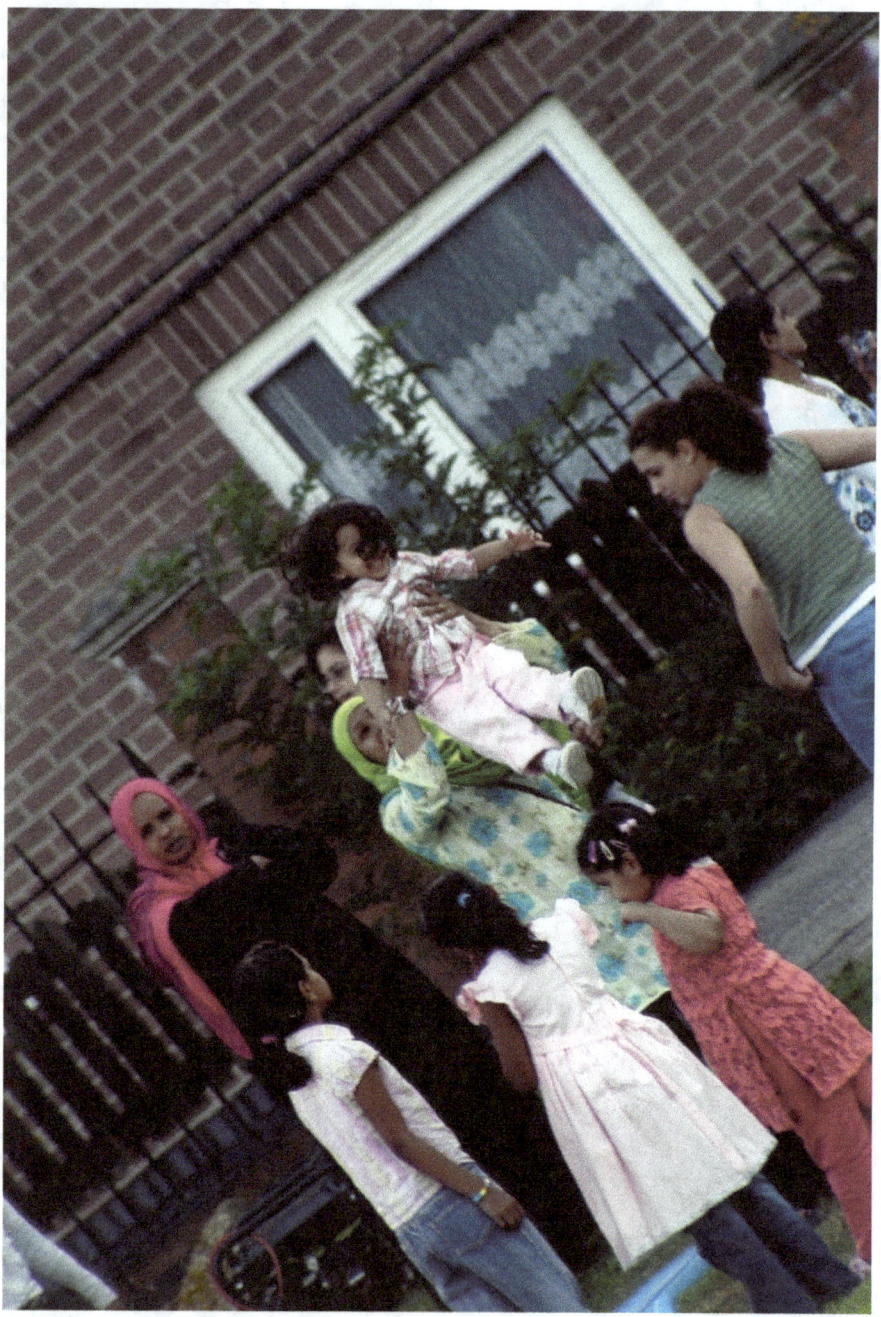

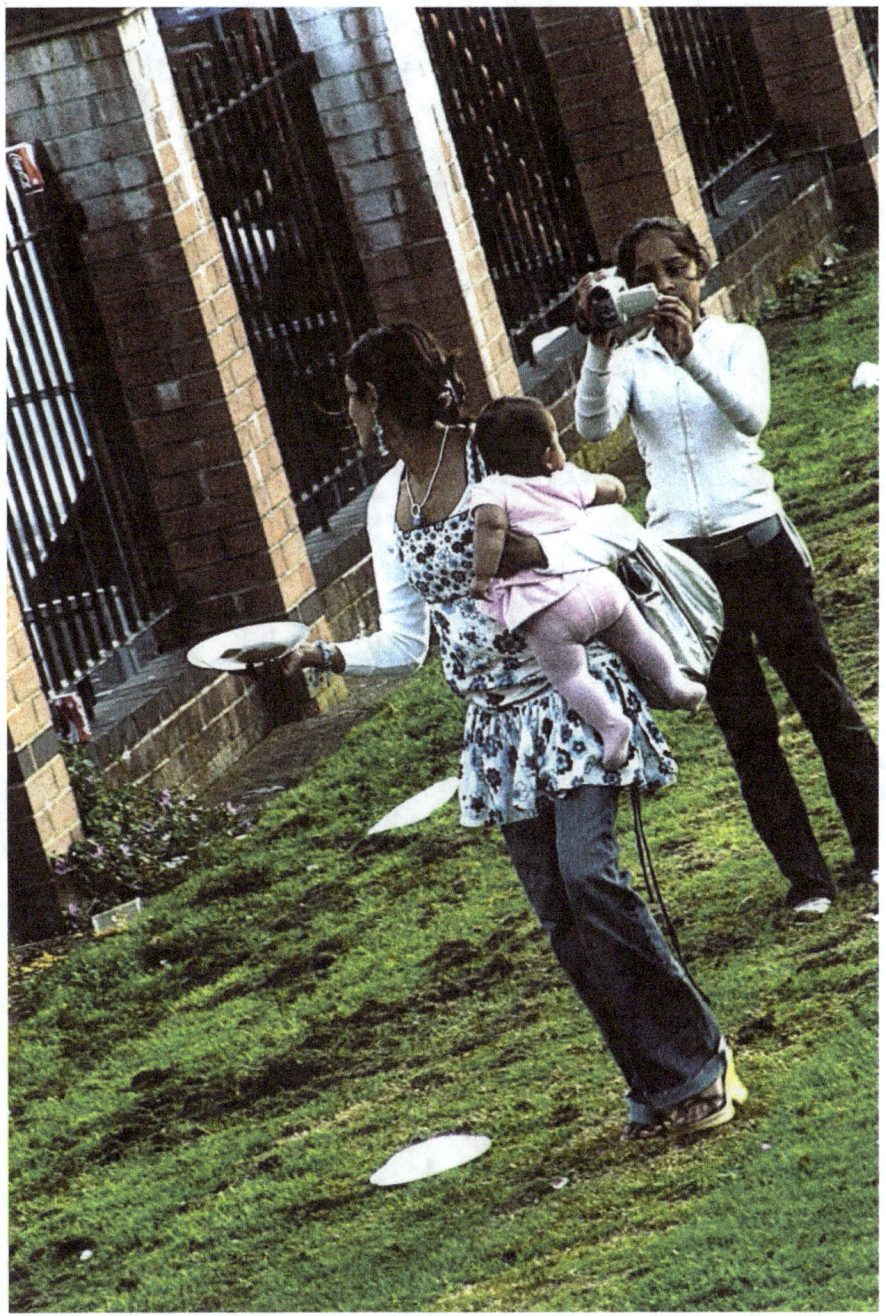

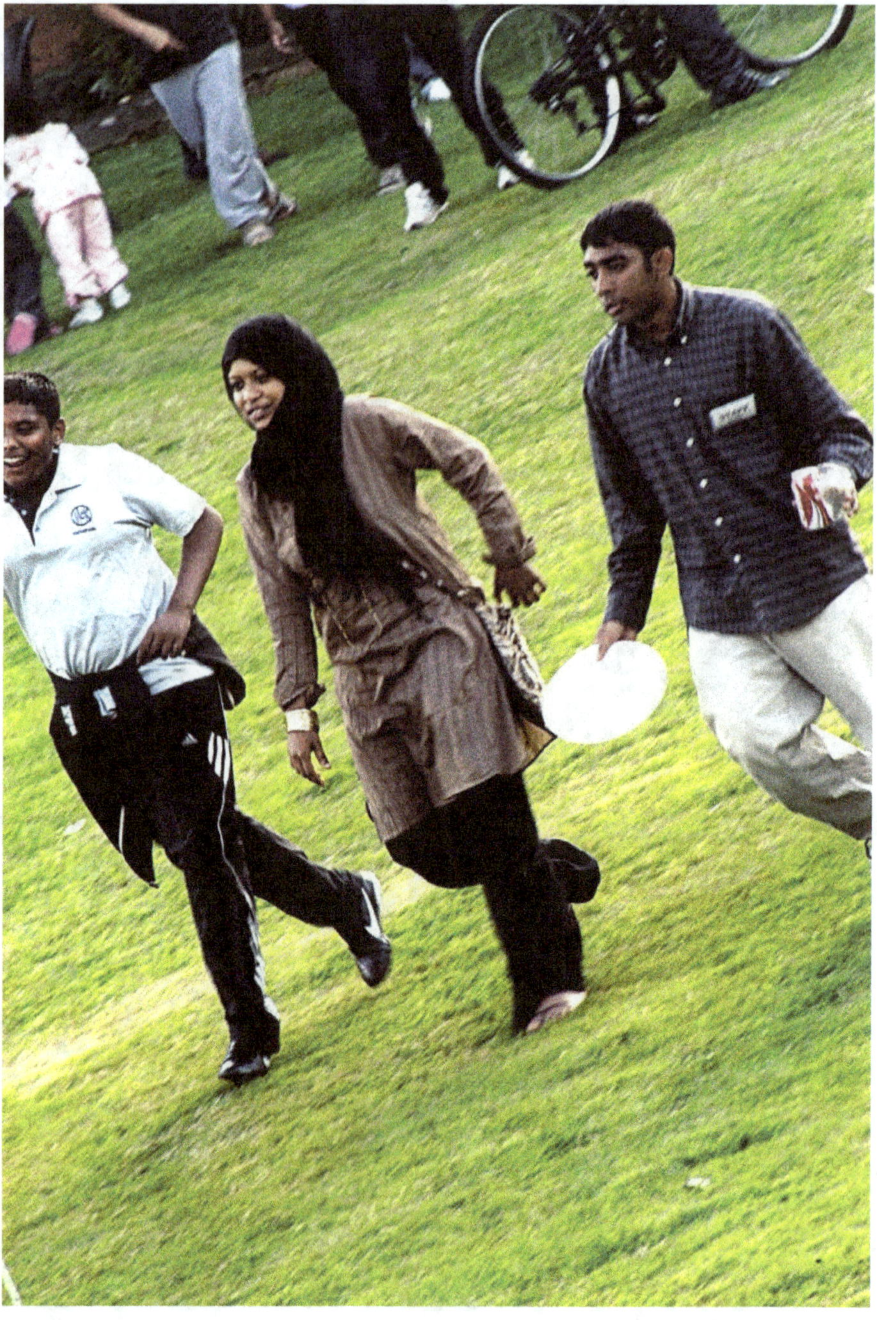

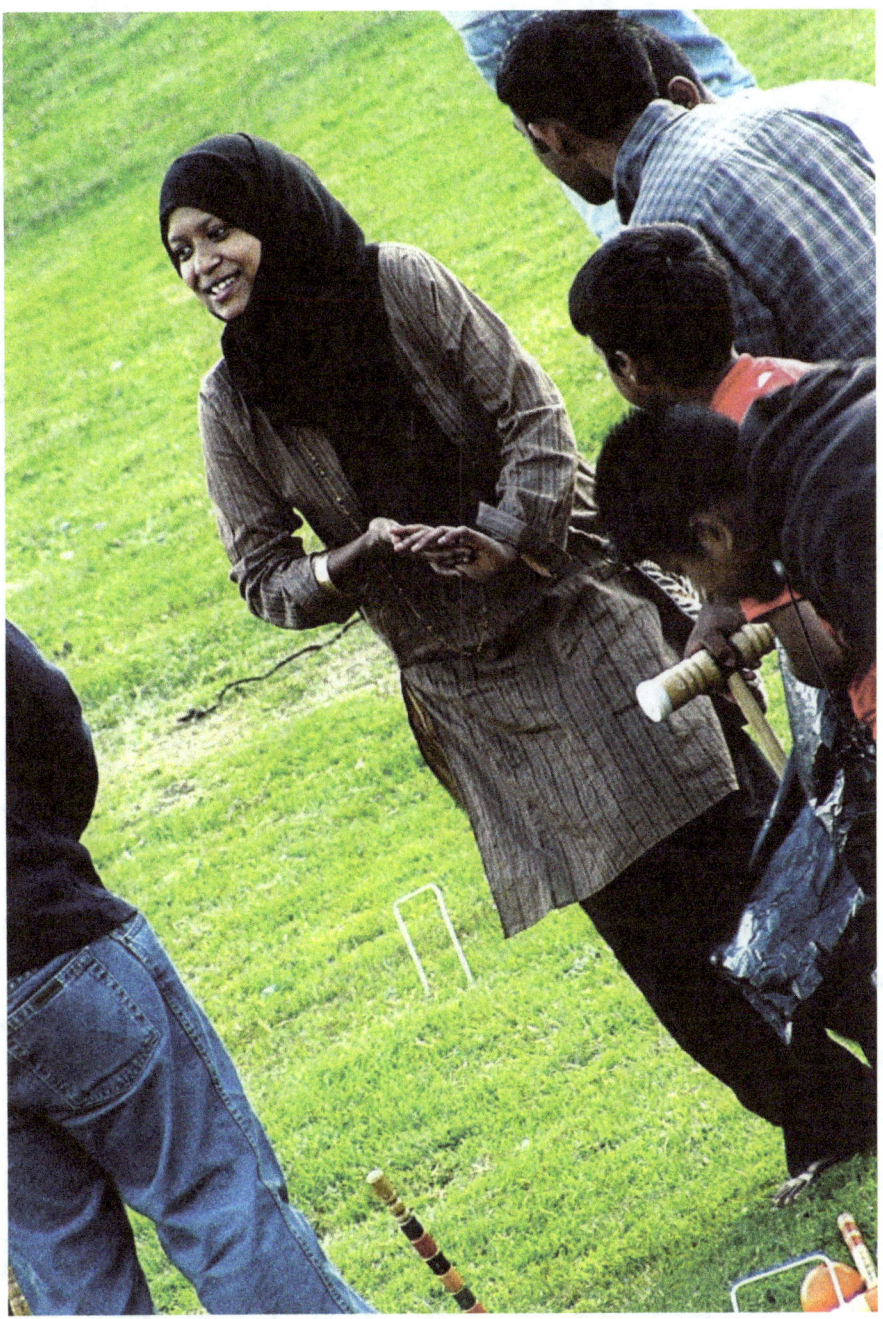

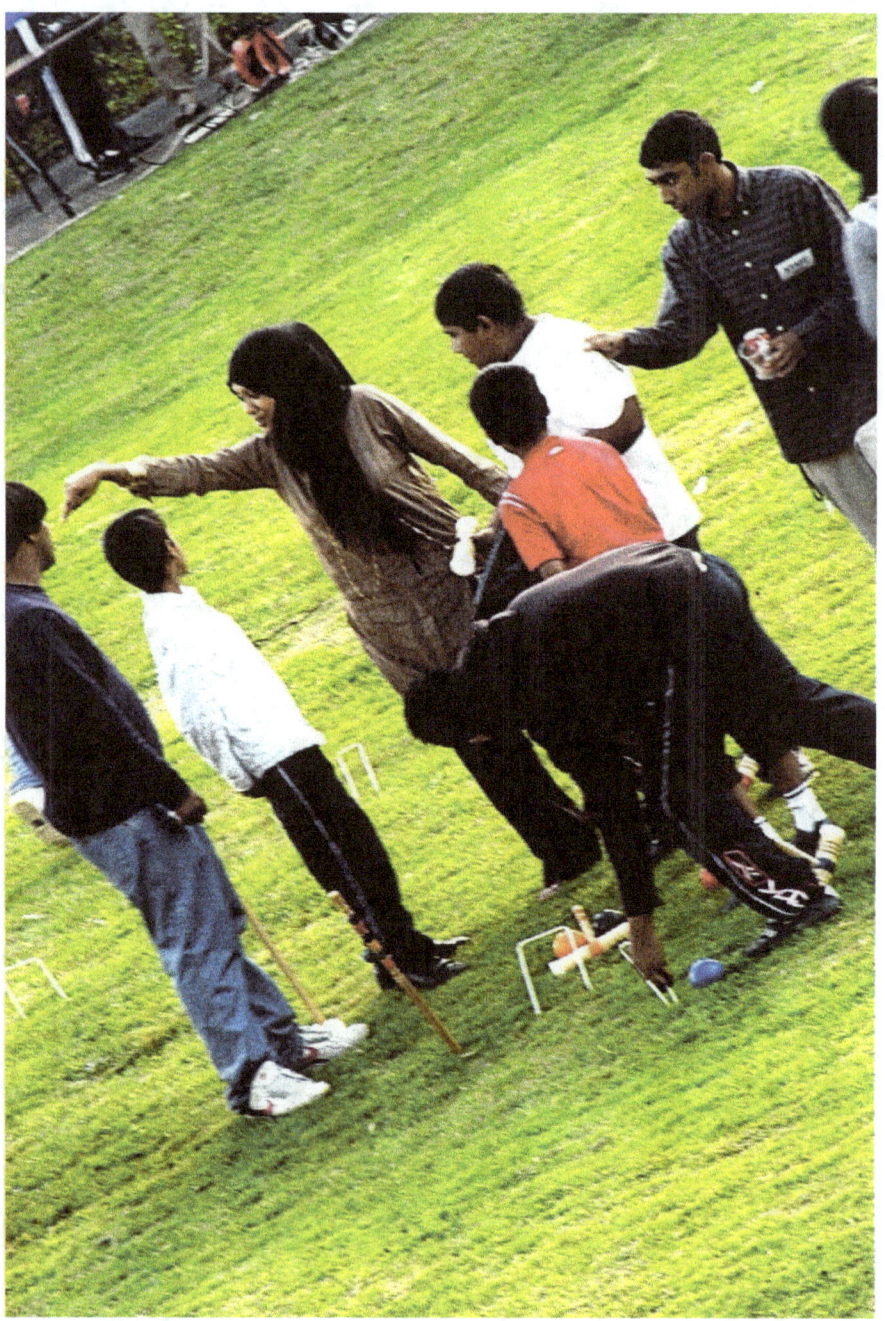

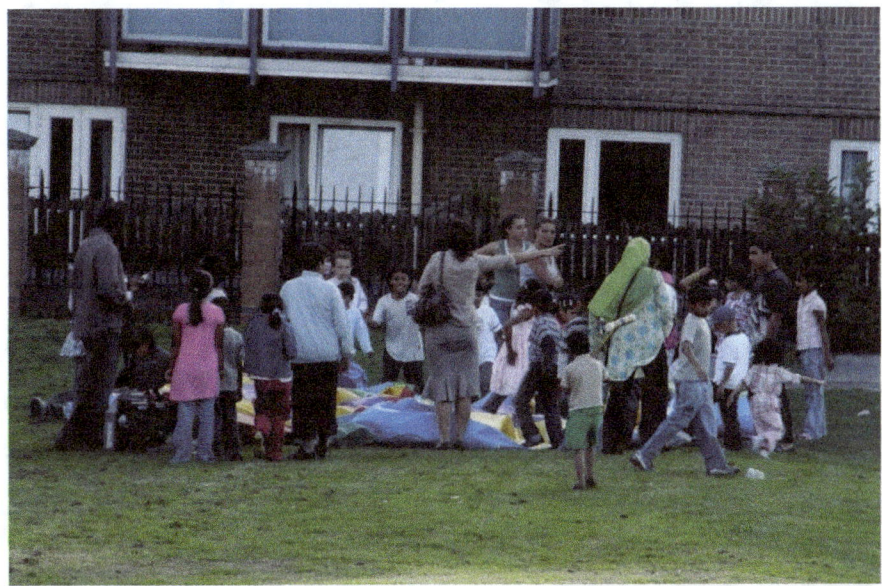

Packing away.

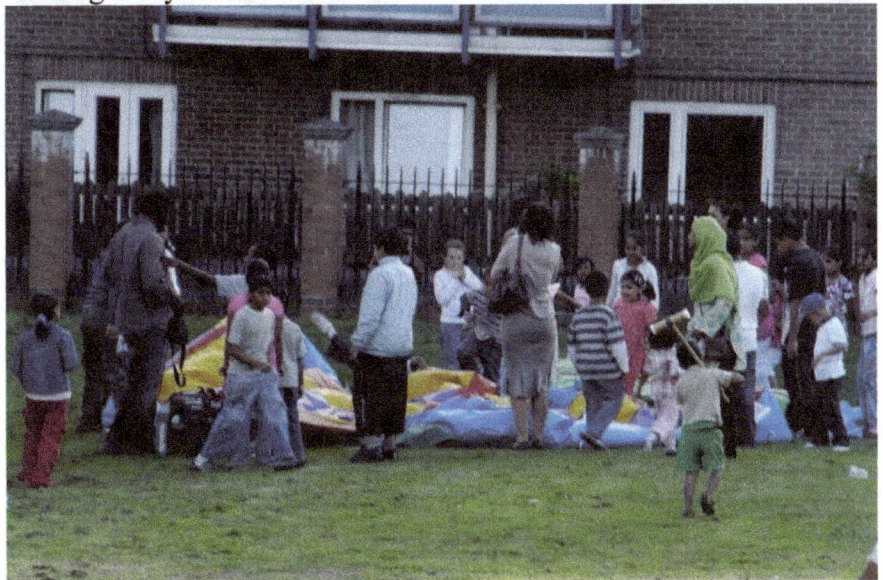

End of the day.

"Documenting the existence of the people of that time"

Here is the rest of the family so far..(in reverse order of release)

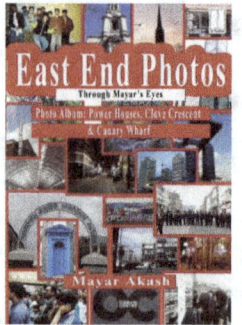

Canary Wharf " Clove Crescent
ISBN:9781910499-634

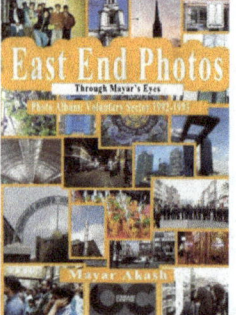

Voluntary Sector 1992-1993
ISBN:9781910499-627

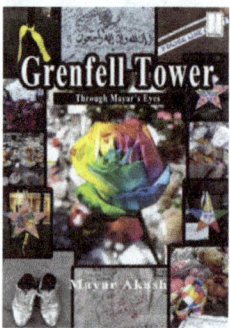

Grenfell Tower
ISBN:9781910499-610

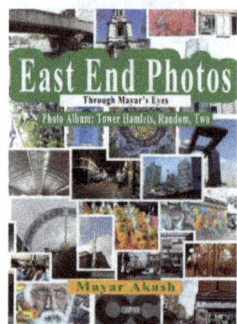

Tower Hamlets random 2
ISBN:9781910499-603

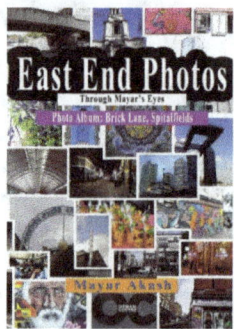

Brick Lane, Spitalfields
ISBN:9781910499-597

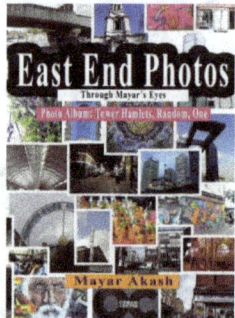

Tower Hamlets random 1
ISBN:9781910499-580

They are available on-line and can be ordered through your local book shops..

www.ingramcontent.com/pod-product-compliance
Lightning Source LLC
Chambersburg PA
CBHW071216220526

45468CB00002B/624